Neither Living

Nor Dead

Neither Living Nor Dead

A Citizen's User's Guide to the United States Constitution

By Jonathan T. Ettinger

"Neither Living Nor Dead – A Citizen's User's Guide to the United States Constitution."

Cover Design by Aaron J. Burch

International Standard Book Number (ISBN): 978-1-456-35052-9

Dedicated to C.E.R.

"…It's all because of you…"

Contents

"[T]he present Constitution is the standard to which we are to cling. Under its banners, bona fide must we combat our political foes -- rejecting all changes but through the channel itself provides for amendments."

--Alexander Hamilton, letter to James Bayard, 1802

Prologue

Before examining the specific contents of the Constitution of the United States, it is important to understand the diametric approaches to misapplying its articles and provisions. People tend to oversimplify and reinterpret things to fit their preconceived and preferred views of how they believe things should be and the Constitution is no exception. What is lacking in this approach is a strict framework of language and law in which to interpret and apply it. Too often, errant understanding of these articles and provisions stems from an incorrect view of the document itself.

The simplest error is one of direct intent. Some will proclaim the Constitution to be "dead" as a means of excusing their choice to blatantly ignore and violate its rules and limitations. Rather than challenging or putting forth any particular interpretation, they will claim that the document is "old" and "archaic" and that this justifies dismissing it entirely. The world is different now, they say. It is a new time and we need new laws. Perhaps they lack an understanding of how the Constitution came to be written and the principles behind it. Perhaps they have specific ends in mind and the only way to achieve them is to dismiss the boundaries set in law over two-hundred years ago. In either case, in these United States, to ignore the Constitution is to ignore the foundation of law itself. The very structure of government is established in the Constitution. How do you justify the existence of government, much less any of its actions, if you deny the document which first established it?

More importantly, how can you expect a standard of law when you remove the central block? Upon what foundation would you say that law and government are built? Do you keep some parts of the Constitution and not others? Who decides?

Why does the age of writing somehow invalidate it? The Bible is far older, yet people still cite it, live by it. In fact, people quite often point to its age as a reason for its validity, not against it. Do ideas become irrelevant as soon as they have aged? If so, how old is too old? When do ideas expire? Is there really nothing that the modern generation can learn from their predecessors? If you understand the Constitution from its philosophical origins, the concepts contained within it, you see the timeless nature of the rights it seeks to protect. There is nothing antiquated about natural rights. In fact, at the time the Constitution was adopted, these rights had only just begun to be identified and considered by mankind, much less established and applied in law as protections for individuals.

Dismissing law as outdated does not remove it; it only marginalizes and avoids it. This approach to law is just a progressive view of law itself. However, progressive, as applied in politics, is a great misnomer. A better term would be modernist. Progressive implies that things are moving forward and improving; but improving builds on what you already have, it doesn't dismiss all things and start over. This isn't an attempt to perfect government, just an excuse to re-invent, re-shape and control it.

What about the clever, modernist claims about a "living" document? This is more of a back-door approach to changing the Constitution without having to bother with following the provided methods for actually changing it. It's far easier to refute claims of antiquity as invalid, so opponents of the Constitution, its would-be assailants, moved to a new tactic of re-interpretation; they re-invent the language. The point of language is to establish common terms to facilitate the expression of ideas. If you do not know, understand or agree on the meaning of words, they cease to be of communicative use. Now, language itself is living. New words come into being and into use all the time. Established words often take on new meanings based on how they've been appropriated at various times. Thus, re-interpreting the Constitution through the eyes and parameters of modern discourse is perfectly allowable, right?

Wrong.

When you write, you choose words to express your ideas. The words chosen have meaning to the author based on the knowledge of the author and the meaning of the words at the time they're written. Placing your own interpretation on someone else's writing changes the meaning entirely. They're not your ideas. They're not your words. A document from the 18th century interpreted by 20th or 21st century linguistic standards makes as much sense as a contemporary writing taken according to 18th century terminology. It's like writing law in current slang. Now, if you choose to apply this to classic literature, that is your choice, but you will entirely miss the intended meaning behind every word, every passage. You do not, however, have the freedom to take this approach with law. Law is a foundational standard. It is meant to be universal. People are not free to interpret law for their selves and selectively apply meaning as it suits them. Any attempt at doing so is just another way of trying to wiggle out of the purposeful and designed boundaries of law to suit the whims of those in power or wishing to be in power. When they can't get what they want within the system, they re-define the system to suit their own ideals. Combine this with actual power in government and we become a nation of men, not laws. Everything is reduced to whim and preference.

There is simply no way to justify such dismissive views. If the Constitution as written is preventing you from accomplishing something, odds are the rest of the people are better off that you cannot get your way. If you still insist on it, that's why the Constitution provides its own process for amending.

Now that we've rejected two modernist approaches at re-inventing the Constitution, we can focus on the simple, straightforward and proper way to interpret the Constitution: read it.

Words have meaning, meaning from the time and mind of the author, not the reader. Sentences have structure. How words are ordered and separated determines their relative meaning to each other. That's it. Know the proper meaning of the words used and how they relate to each other.

We the People of the United States, in Order to form a more perfect Union, establish Justice, insure domestic Tranquility, provide for the common defence, promote the general Welfare, and secure the Blessings of Liberty to ourselves and our Posterity, do ordain and establish this Constitution for the United States of America.

Nearly every American has seen or heard those words at least once. Do they really read them, though? Do they know what the words mean, or how they apply to law? First and foremost: what's a preamble?

A preamble is an introductory statement; a preface. The point of the preamble is to say "this is why we wrote the following." In fact, that's all it is. It starts "We the People of the United States," ends "…do ordain and establish this Constitution for the United States of America" and in between is a list of reasons why they did it.

We the People of the United States

It does not say "We the States" or "We the Legislatures" or "We the Congress." From the very start, the authors make clear that the power and authority for this Constitution comes from the people. However, they do not call themselves "the People of the United States of America" or "Americans," rather, "the People of the United States." This is significant because it also shows an emphasis on the States themselves, as opposed to any central authority. The people of the States did not come together to dissolve their various State ties and unite as "Americans." These are people, via their representatives, from each State, uniting as people, and States, for a common purpose. It is not "The United States," a singular entity, but "the United States," a unified group of States.

in Order to form a more perfect Union

The first, and arguably most important, reason the people came together to draft this document was to form a more perfect Union. What does that mean? It means that, first and foremost, they knew that perfection was unattainable, that no matter how you craft a "utopian ideal," by nature it is not possible. Even Sir Thomas More knew that when he coined the term. Utopia comes from the Greek and means "no place." The point of More's book was that such a place could not be.

The Union, of course, speaks to a joining together of the States, a united front, as opposed to an amalgam, which would take the many States and make a new identity from the parts. A Union allows the parts to remain individual and distinct, not to sublimate their properties to each other or the new identity. It is a joining, not a mixing. Like all Unions, the member parts are not bound to stay, but may separate if they so choose.

Under the Articles of Confederation, the States seemed to some to be united in name only, thus the Constitution was written to bring them together more tightly with the hope of improving their function and relationships.

establish Justice, insure domestic Tranquility

There is not much point to calling yourself any kind of united anything, confederation or otherwise, if you cannot settle disputes and keep the peace. Again, this is a point where the Articles of Confederation were considered to be deficient. The authors of the Constitution sought to establish and maintain peace and justice between the States.

provide for the common defence

One of the primary reasons for uniting the States in any form is to provide for defense, to aid each other in times of conflict and crisis. The ability to do this is predicated on the closeness of the relationships between those States, hence the need for a stronger system to unite them.

promote the general Welfare

The first instance of the phrase "general Welfare" within the Constitution; as written, the point of this phrase was to promote, meaning help or advance, the general, meaning overall, welfare, meaning well-being. The objective was to form a system which allowed the people to flourish and thus allow room for their overall well-being. It was never meant to be welfare as we have egregiously come to know it from the 20th Century onward.

Even if you claim welfare to equate to alms or charity, it distinctly says promote, not provide, so, at most, one purpose of this Constitution is to promote charity, not to directly provide it. Unfortunately, what is more commonly claimed and put into practice is the very antithesis of this, that it is somehow the responsibility of this new government to be the source of charitable giving to take care of the people. Such a view, of course, wholly ignores that these people are citizens of their own States and if any government is to take on such a responsibility, it is those States, not any central government.

and secure the Blessings of Liberty to ourselves and our Posterity

It is with an eye to liberty and freedom, not just for their own selves but for the generations which follow, that these concepts are put down in writing and that this new union is formed. It took only seven phrases into the document to not just mention liberty, but to regard it as a blessing. Liberty, ultimately, is freedom from captivity or control. The point of this document and the government it forms is to secure that freedom for the people of these States and all those who come after them.

Unfortunately, this idea, both the esteem for liberty and the necessity of securing it, is too often taken for granted at best or wholly disavowed at worst. Contemporary practices too often do more to infringe on liberty and burden posterity. Any time a new law adds to the power of government, it furthers diminishes the liberty of the individual. Any time government spends into an ever-expanding mountain of debt and obligation, it weakens the people today and burdens the people tomorrow. This is exactly what the authors sought to avoid.

do ordain and establish this Constitution for the United States of America

The closing phrase is the action taken. They told you who were doing it, the reasons why, then what they did. They ordained and established this Constitution, this governing document of legal formation. They did it for the United States of America. It is a Constitution for the United States, not of them. This shows the Constitution was written for the States, to

16

bring them together, as opposed to being a document of or about the United States which could be misconstrued as creating those States. Again, they recognize the sovereignty of the many States they are there to represent. When you look at a map of Europe, you don't see one color encompassing the entirety that is the European Union. You see each state distinctly identified from the others. Why, then, do we insist on viewing the United States of America as The United States of America and diminishing the individual States to nothing more than partitioned sections instead of distinct and sovereign States?

Now that you understand the preamble part by part, section by section, what is its application to law? It has none. The actual legal structure in the Constitution, as with other legal documents, starts with Article I. The preamble, as noted earlier, is purely explanative. There is not one phrase of it that is legally binding in any way. It simply explains the intent of the governing structure and laws which follow it in the document. You cannot point to the "welfare clause" here and claim it as a power of the federal government because it is just not so.

What it is, and can be, is a helpful guide to understanding the intent of the Constitution when examining one of the Articles or their sections. It is easier to understand the meaning of the legal terms when you understand the intent behind their writing. That is why the preamble is there. It is not meant to simply be poetic oratory, nor a grand and sweeping rhetorical proclamation. However, not one word of it carries the weight of law nor enumerates any kind of power.

Article I

Section. 1.

All legislative Powers herein granted shall be vested in a Congress of the United States, which shall consist of a Senate and House of Representatives.

All legislative powers, meaning all, without exception, are in the Congress, herein created and consisting of a Senate and House of Representatives. This means no one from the judiciary or executive branch has the power to legislate. No president can create law, even by executive order. No office or position under executive authority can create law. The EPA can make rules over its own internal operations, but nothing with authority over anyone not employed within the EPA. No court can create law through its decisions. If either the court or the executive were meant to have legislative authority, they would have been provided such. Moreover, Congress is not empowered here to delegate such legislative power, nor assumed to have the power to delegate. The Constitution declares that all legislative powers granted by this Constitution are to be vested in Congress and only Congress.

Section. 2.

The House of Representatives shall be composed of Members chosen every second Year by the People of the several States, and the Electors in each State shall have the Qualifications requisite for Electors of the most numerous Branch of the State Legislature.

Members of the House shall be chosen every two years. To qualify to vote to choose them, you must meet the qualifications to vote to choose the members of the larger branch of the State Legislature. Indirectly, the States set voting eligibility for choosing Members of the House of Representatives by setting the same for their own State Legislatures.

No Person shall be a Representative who shall not have attained to the Age of twenty five Years, and been seven Years a Citizen of the United States, and who shall not, when elected, be an Inhabitant of that State in which he shall be chosen.

18

To be a Representative in the House, you must be at least twenty five years old, been a citizen of the United States for at least seven years and at time of election be an inhabitant of the state in which you are chosen. An inhabitant is one who inhabits, a person who lives or dwells in a place. It does not say resident or legal resident. It does not say must be of a certain residency status with the state. It says you must, when elected, be an inhabitant, that you must live there at all, not that you must be there permanently or have been there for a considerable amount of time as with a resident, or a legal resident, one recognized by State authority as being a resident. Moreover, it does not say you must live, reside or inhabit within the district from which you are elected. Districting is a matter of electoral convenience, not geographic identification or specification. The idea that you must be from District 5 to run for the District 5 seat has been contrived through years of tradition and party politics, nothing to do with law or legitimacy. A Representative is there to protect the rights of all the people of his State, not to curry special favors for the few within a semi-arbitrary political construct called a district.

Representatives and direct Taxes shall be apportioned among the several States which may be included within this Union, according to their respective Numbers, which shall be determined by adding to the whole Number of free Persons, including those bound to Service for a Term of Years, and excluding Indians not taxed, three fifths of all other Persons.

Representation and direct taxation shall be determined by apportionment among the several States which may be included within this Union. In short, a State's representation in the House and any taxation on the people of the State, by this new government, shall be allocated through proportional distribution by population. This population is set by counting the whole of all free Persons, including those bound to service, those being indentured servants and the like, and three fifths of all other Persons, excluding any Indians not being taxed for one reason or another.

This is a part which often raises ire. People focus on the three fifths while wholly overlooking the word Persons. Nothing in this passage specifically sets any Person as less than another. Nothing in this passage decrees more or fewer rights for one Person than another. In fact, what it actually does is recognize everyone as Persons. So, why the three fifths rule? This is representation according to population, a head count of Persons within a State. Some States at the time were far larger in population due to the numerous slaves there. If you count these slaves as property, they are not Persons and do not count toward your population at all. If you count them as Persons, each counts as only three fifths of another Person in order to off-set the numeric disparity. After all, slaves are not recognized by the States as equal with all others, so to count them in regard to this apportionment would be skewing the legitimacy of the count as the full citizens of that State would be allocated far more power numerically than Persons in a State with few or no slaves.

The compromise reached was that slaves would be recognized as Persons for the purposes of apportionment, as opposed to not at all, but only three fifths of them would add to the total population, so as to recognize them within the State but not completely skew the power balance between States. At no point does it outright state that one person is only three fifths of another person by any sort of designation or reasoning. It says nothing about the Persons themselves, only about how they are to be counted.

One final note of importance here is that taxation is to be done according to that same population count. The total taxes paid by a State shall be done in a manner in accordance with the population of that State. While it does not say the people are to be taxed directly in equal measure per person, the amount taxed per State is determined by the population count so that the taxation assessed per person is equal between the States. Thus, taxation is to be done according to population. While the State itself may then assess this tax to its people according to its own laws, the taxes owed by a State to this new government shall be in equal measure according to population. No other method of taxation on the States or people is allowed.

The actual Enumeration shall be made within three Years after the first Meeting of the Congress of the United States, and within every subsequent Term of ten Years, in such Manner as they shall by Law direct.

The enumeration of the population shall be counted within three years after the first meeting of the Congress and within every ten years thereafter in such a manner as Congress shall direct by law. It doesn't

20

say count every ten years, but within ten years of the previous count. We could conduct a census every year if Congress directed. At the least, we could count on odd years, between House elections, and change Congressional apportionment every two years rather than setting it for ten years at a time.

The Number of Representatives shall not exceed one for every thirty Thousand, but each State shall have at Least one Representative; and until such enumeration shall be made, the State of New Hampshire shall be entitled to chuse three, Massachusetts eight, Rhode-Island and Providence Plantations one, Connecticut five, New-York six, New Jersey four, Pennsylvania eight, Delaware one, Maryland six, Virginia ten, North Carolina five, South Carolina five, and Georgia three.

Representatives shall not exceed one for every thirty thousand in population. In other words, you may never have one representative per population of less than thirty thousand people, but you may have one for more than thirty thousand. This is meant to control the size of the House. Until that first enumeration is made, each state is entitled to representation as prescribed here.

When vacancies happen in the Representation from any State, the Executive Authority thereof shall issue Writs of Election to fill such Vacancies.

Should a vacancy occur in the House, the Executive Authority of that state shall call for an election to fill it.

The House of Representatives shall chuse their Speaker and other Officers; and shall have the sole Power of Impeachment.

The House shall choose from among its members their Speaker and other officers. It does not specify any officer other than the Speaker. However, it should be noted that modern designations along majority and minority terms are set with political affiliation by party under a House divided and controlled by two parties. No mention is made here of dividing along political or party lines for any purpose, but the House does have power to establish officers and select them. It also does not say the Speaker is meant to be a permanent title for any one individual rather than someone chosen to chair the meetings. If you watch House proceedings, various people act as Speaker while the House is in session, as they are allowed. There is no call for any one person to permanently hold the title of Speaker of the House.

The House also has the sole power of impeachment. No official of the United States may be impeached anywhere but by the House of Representatives. Impeachment is the accusing of and charging with improper conduct. In other words, it is the House who brings charges against an individual for their conduct.

Section. 3.

The Senate of the United States shall be composed of two Senators from each State, chosen by the Legislature thereof for six Years; and each Senator shall have one Vote.

The Senate shall be composed of two Senators from each State, chosen by State Legislatures for terms of six years, and each Senator shall have one vote. Section 2 established the chamber for the people and Section 3 established the chamber for the States. Each house is established and designed with a specific purpose in mind. The intent here was not only a compromise to have one house by population and the other by equal representation, but also to have the house by population represent the people and the other to represent the States. It was understood from the start that the people create the governments, that they created the States and that the States come together to create this government. A Senate chosen by Legislatures represents those Legislatures, those States, to protect their power and interests from the federal government. In short, it is up to the Senate to protect the rights of the States as the House protects the rights of the people.

Immediately after they shall be assembled in Consequence of the first Election, they shall be divided as equally as may be into three Classes. The Seats of the Senators of the first Class shall be vacated at the Expiration of the second Year, of the second Class at the Expiration of the fourth Year, and of the third Class at the Expiration of the sixth Year, so that one third may be chosen every second Year; and if Vacancies happen by Resignation, or otherwise, during the Recess of the Legislature of any State, the Executive thereof may make

temporary Appointments until the next Meeting of the Legislature, which shall then fill such Vacancies.

The first Senate shall be divided among three classes so that one class expires in two years, the second in four years and the third in six years, after which, each class will serve for six years with one third of the Senate expiring every two years. If Senate vacancies occur during the recess of any Legislature of any State, the Executive of that State may make temporary appointments until the next meeting of the Legislature.

No Person shall be a Senator who shall not have attained to the Age of thirty Years, and been nine Years a Citizen of the United States, and who shall not, when elected, be an Inhabitant of that State for which he shall be chosen.

Similar to the House in Section 2, to be a Senator, you must be at least thirty years old, been a citizen of the United States for at least nine years and at time of election be an inhabitant of the State for which you are chosen.

The Vice President of the United States shall be President of the Senate, but shall have no Vote, unless they be equally divided.

The Vice President of the United States is to serve as President of the Senate, meaning be in charge of it and chair its meetings, but has no vote in the Senate unless they be equally divided, at which point the President of the Senate casts the tie-breaking vote.

The Senate shall chuse their other Officers, and also a President pro tempore, in the Absence of the Vice President, or when he shall exercise the Office of President of the United States.

Like the House, the Senate has power to create and choose its officers. In addition to its own officers, the Senate shall select a President pro tempore to act as President of the Senate in the Absence of the Vice President or when the Vice President shall exercise the Office of President of the United States. Note that it does not appoint any permanent title of President pro tempore. In fact, pro tempore means temporary. Much like the Speaker of the House, the President pro tempore is meant to be chosen from among the Senate when it convenes. Unlike the Speaker, the President pro tempore is meant to be named sparingly, when necessary, otherwise, it is the job of the Vice President of the United States to serve as President of the Senate. The President pro tempore is meant to fill in only at times when the Vice President is absent or making use of the Office of President of the United States.

The Senate shall have the sole Power to try all Impeachments. When sitting for that Purpose, they shall be on Oath or Affirmation. When the President of the United States is tried, the Chief Justice shall preside: And no Person shall be convicted without the Concurrence of two thirds of the Members present.

When the House has brought impeachment against someone, they are tried only in the Senate. When assembled for the purpose of an impeachment trial, they shall be on Oath or Affirmation and conduct themselves as a court. When it is the President of the United States who is tried, the Chief Justice shall preside. No person shall be convicted in these trials without having so done by two thirds of the members present. It does not, however, mandate any number for quorum to hold these trials, only that two thirds of the members assembled must agree to have a guilty verdict.

Judgment in Cases of Impeachment shall not extend further than to removal from Office, and disqualification to hold and enjoy any Office of honor, Trust or Profit under the United States: but the Party convicted shall nevertheless be liable and subject to Indictment, Trial, Judgment and Punishment, according to Law.

Impeachment trials cannot punish beyond removal from office and disqualification to hold and enjoy any Office of honor, trust or profit under the United States. A person found guilty may only be punished so far as removal from Office and disqualification from holding other Offices under the United States. It does not say such persons cannot hold Office within a State or lower government. In fact, the point is that removal and disqualification is the most this trial may punish someone under impeachment. However, any convicted party is still liable and subject to indictment, trial, judgment and punishment according to law. Such punishments just cannot be meted out by the Senate.

Section. 4.

The Times, Places and Manner of holding Elections for Senators and Representatives, shall be prescribed in each State by the Legislature thereof; but the Congress may at any time by Law make or alter such Regulations, except as to the Places of chusing Senators.

Each State shall make its own laws for the election of Representatives and selection of Senators. However, Congress reserves the ability, by law, to make or alter such regulations, except the places of choosing Senators. This is to say that Congress can oversee and alter, by law, all manner of choosing its own members except so far as changing where Senators are chosen, in and by the Legislature. State election law for these Offices is superseded by this section.

The Congress shall assemble at least once in every Year, and such Meeting shall be on the first Monday in December, unless they shall by Law appoint a different Day.

The Congress, the legislature comprising both the House and Senate, is to assemble no less than once every year. If only meeting once, it shall be on the first Monday in December unless the Congress, by law, appoints a different day. The important part here is not whether the Congress meets in December or not, but that it is not required to meet more than once a year. If the majority of governance happened at the State level, there would be little reason for Congress to convene and it would only do so at certain times for specific reasons. Mandating that it must meet at least once a year simply keeps the body functioning and in existence.

Section. 5.

Each House shall be the Judge of the Elections, Returns and Qualifications of its own Members, and a Majority of each shall constitute a Quorum to do Business; but a smaller Number may adjourn from day to day, and may be authorized to compel the Attendance of absent Members, in such Manner, and under such Penalties as each House may provide.

Each House has final say on seating its members, being the final judge on the elections, returns and qualifications of same. A majority of each House shall constitute a Quorum to do business. However, a smaller number than that quorum may adjourn from day to day, which is to say compel adjournment by leaving less than a majority present, and may also compel the attendance of absent members, as its House rules provide, to establish quorum and do business.

Each House may determine the Rules of its Proceedings, punish its Members for disorderly Behaviour, and, with the Concurrence of two thirds, expel a Member.

Each House may set its own rules, may punish members for disorderly behaviour and, with two thirds in agreement, expel a member.

Each House shall keep a Journal of its Proceedings, and from time to time publish the same, excepting such Parts as may in their Judgment require Secrecy; and the Yeas and Nays of the Members of either House on any question shall, at the Desire of one fifth of those Present, be entered on the Journal.

Each House must keep a journal of its proceedings and, from time to time, must publish the same. Each House may decide that some things are of such high secrecy so as to be left out of the journal, though this does not stop members who disagree from making those matters public, lest House rules say otherwise. If one fifth of the members present desire it, the Yeas and Nays of any question before the House shall also be included in the journal.

Neither House, during the Session of Congress, shall, without the Consent of the other, adjourn for more than three days, nor to any other Place than that in which the two Houses shall be sitting.

While Congress is in session, if one House wishes to adjourn to another location or for a period of time longer than three days, it must have the consent of the other House. Adjournment is not just an action of meeting time, in session or not, but also of location. The entire Congress could adjourn to, as in move to, a place other than the Capitol if both Houses consent.

Section. 6.

The Senators and Representatives shall receive a Compensation for their Services, to be ascertained by Law, and paid out of the Treasury of the United States. They shall in all Cases, except Treason, Felony and Breach of the Peace, be privileged from Arrest during their Attendance at the Session of their respective Houses, and in going to and returning from the same; and for any Speech or Debate in either House, they shall not be questioned in any other Place.

The Senators and Representatives shall be paid out of Treasury funds. They are also privileged from arrest during their attendance at session, going to and from session, and for any speech or debate given in session in either House, except in matters of Treason, Felony or Breach of the Peace. Members of Congress are free to express themselves while serving in Congress, except for major offenses.

No Senator or Representative shall, during the Time for which he was elected, be appointed to any civil Office under the Authority of the United States, which shall have been created, or the Emoluments whereof shall have been encreased during such time; and no Person holding any Office under the United States, shall be a Member of either House during his Continuance in Office.

No member of Congress shall simultaneously hold a civil Office under the authority of the United States if that Office shall have been created or had its pay increased during that member's time in Congress. This is a way of trying to keep Congress from creating jobs for itself or giving itself pay raises. Moreover, no person shall simultaneously hold any Office under the United States and also be a member of Congress. It can only be one or the other.

Section. 7.

All Bills for raising Revenue shall originate in the House of Representatives; but the Senate may propose or concur with Amendments as on other Bills.

Any bill to raise revenue, to gain money for this government, to monetarily increase the government, shall originate in the House of Representatives. However, the Senate may propose or agree to such measures with amendments as on other bills.

Every Bill which shall have passed the House of Representatives and the Senate, shall, before it become a Law, be presented to the President of the United States: If he approve he shall sign it, but if not he shall return it, with his Objections to that House in which it shall have originated, who shall enter the Objections at large on their Journal, and proceed to reconsider it. If after such Reconsideration two thirds of that House shall agree to pass the Bill, it shall be sent, together with the Objections, to the other House, by which it shall likewise be reconsidered, and if approved by two thirds of that House, it shall become a Law. But in all such Cases the Votes of both Houses shall be determined by yeas and Nays, and the Names of the Persons voting for and against the Bill shall be entered on the Journal of each House respectively. If any Bill shall not be returned by the President within ten Days (Sundays excepted) after it shall have been presented to him, the Same shall be a Law, in like Manner as if he had signed it, unless the Congress by their Adjournment prevent its Return, in which Case it shall not be a Law.

Every bill passed by both Houses must be sent to the President for approval. If he does not sign it, it goes back to the House where it originated, with the President's objections, the objections shall go in the journal of that House and the bill shall be reconsidered. If two thirds of that House pass the bill, it is sent to the other House where it also requires approval by two thirds. If approved by two thirds of each House, it shall become law. Whenever the President sends back a bill and both houses approve by two thirds, the Yeas and Nays of each House shall be recorded in their respective journals, not just in total, but by name of persons voting for or against.

If any bill is not returned by the President within ten days of its receipt (excluding Sundays), it shall be law, the same as though he had signed it, unless he is prevented by the adjournment of Congress from returning it.

Every Order, Resolution, or Vote to which the Concurrence of the Senate and House of Representatives may be necessary (except on a question of Adjournment) shall be presented to the President of the United States; and before the Same shall take Effect, shall be approved by him, or being disapproved by him, shall be repassed by two thirds of the Senate and House of Representatives, according to the Rules and Limitations prescribed in the Case of a Bill.

Every measure requiring an agreement reached by the Congress, except the matter of its own adjournment, shall be presented to the President for approval before taking effect. If not approved by him, it shall require passage by two thirds of the Senate and House of Representatives. In the case of a bill, a proposed statute or law, that passage must be done according to the rules and limitations prescribed.

Section. 8.

The Congress shall have Power To lay and collect Taxes, Duties, Imposts and Excises, to pay the Debts and provide for the common Defence and general Welfare of the United States; but all Duties, Imposts and Excises shall be uniform throughout the United States;

Congress has the power to lay and collect taxes, duties, imposts and excises for the purposes of paying the debts and providing for the common defense and general welfare of the United States. However, all duties (tax on imports or exports), imposts (customs duties) and excises (internal taxes on commodities) shall be uniform throughout the United States. No preference shall be given to any place or person within the United States.

This has got to be one of the more oft-cited lines in the entire document; the so-called "welfare clause." Whereas the preamble states a reason of "promote the general Welfare," this section says "provide for the...general Welfare." However, this is not a granted power, nor an imposed requirement, to provide that welfare. The specific power here is one of taxation. Providing for the general Welfare is a reason given as valid cause for taxation. The Congress is still limited by the rest of the document and all laws from under it on what matters it may undertake.

In essence, this government has two main duties, defense and welfare. Each of those is further specified within the Constitution as to their limitations. This section merely provides that Congress is authorized to tax for the purposes of defense and welfare. In no way does this grant carte blanche power to Congress, under the guise of the "general Welfare," to create whatever laws or offices it so desires. It certainly does not say "Congress has the power to tax whomever and however for the purposes of redistributing the wealth to others for the paying of alms or charity." If "pay debts," "provide Defence" and "provide Welfare" were meant as additional, separate, specific powers, they would have been listed that way, like the powers which follow in this Section.

At its most extreme, you could argue the Congress has power to keep taxing unceasingly in the name of "general Welfare," not just for specific purposes, but it is still limited on its exercisable powers. This would result in a Congress which keeps collecting money that it cannot spend without naming the specific power and means. If Congress has the power and ability "A," then it has the power to tax for the purpose of ability "A." A broad, general claim to taxation ability with limited spending ability is either pointlessly banal or financially burdensome. Why keep taxing when spending power is limited?

To borrow Money on the credit of the United States;

Congress alone has the power to borrow money on the credit of the Unites States. No State, Office or individual within the United States may borrow money on the credit worthiness and promise to repay of the United States itself.

To regulate Commerce with foreign Nations, and among the several States, and with the Indian Tribes;

Congress has authority to direct commerce with foreign nations, among the States and with the Indian Tribes. Note that it says among the States, not inside them. It is also treating the State in its proper context of a political entity and treating Virginia and Connecticut the same as it does France and England. For years this meant the States could not set rules for commerce with foreign nations or Indian Tribes nor set rules to discriminate one State from another. That was the entire point. Chief Justice John Marshall upheld this view in the 1824 decision *Gibbons v. Ogden*. It's only been since the late 19th century, and especially since the 1930s, that it's been re-interpreted and re-imagined to mean Congress can make rules and regulations over any business and claim authority simply because the company and goods are considered to affect interstate commerce. This broad interpretation runs contrary to law. In the opinion of Supreme Court nominee Robert Bork, the lack of its use in such way for the nation's first century shows it was not meant to be. The point of regulating commerce is to keep it uniform, to not let States engage in economic warfare with each other, not to control business.

To establish an uniform Rule of Naturalization, and uniform Laws on the subject of Bankruptcies throughout the United States;

Congress has the power to set uniform rule for foreign citizens to be admitted or adopted as a citizen here as well as uniform bankruptcy laws throughout the United States.

To coin Money, regulate the Value thereof, and of foreign Coin, and fix the Standard of Weights and Measures;

Only Congress may coin money, set its inherent value, its value in relation to foreign money and set the singular standard for weights and measures. This last part is included here specifically because there needed to be a uniform standard for weighing gold so that its amount or weight would correspond with monetary values. It is up to the Congress alone to coin money and determine its value in relation to commodity backing and foreign exchange.

To provide for the Punishment of counterfeiting the Securities and current Coin of the United States;

A specific provision to ensure Congress has the unquestionable authority to punish counterfeiters of the evidences of debt and current coin of the United States, a protection of the previous power on money.

To establish Post Offices and post Roads;

Congress has the power to establish offices and roads for mail service.

To promote the Progress of Science and useful Arts, by securing for limited Times to Authors and Inventors the exclusive Right to their respective Writings and Discoveries;

Congress, for the purpose of promoting the progress of science and useful arts, may secure, for limited times, the rights to writings and discoveries to their respective authors and inventors. It states plainly, these rights are for writing and discoveries and that exclusivity is for limited times only. There never was meant to be perpetual exclusivity by anyone for anything. If you write or invent something, you have so long before others can copy and use it. You cannot claim something as your creation and hold absolute control over its use for all time.

This is also the first time the term "right" has been used in this Constitution. It simultaneously protects and limits an individual right to property. It extends the right of property, of ownership, beyond the tangible and into ideas, but only for a limited time. It does not change the concept of an individual right, only gives temporary claim to ideas as property, to which there is an inherent, individual right.

To constitute Tribunals inferior to the supreme Court;

Congress may create varying courts inferior to the supreme Court [sic] but it is not granted exclusivity to the creation of all courts and handling of all legal matters.

To define and punish Piracies and Felonies committed on the high Seas, and Offences against the Law of Nations;

Congress has authority to define and punish piracies and felonies committed on the high seas. It also has authority to define and punish offenses against the Law of Nations. As Jon Roland of the Constitution Society noted in 1998; "It is important to understand what is and is not included in the term of art "law of nations", and not confuse it with "international law". They are not the same thing. The phrase "law of nations" is a direct translation of the Latin *jus gentium*, which means the underlying principles of right and justice among nations, and during the founding era was not considered the same as the "laws", that is, the body of treaties and conventions between nations, the *jus inter gentes*, which, combined with *jus gentium*, comprise "international law". The distinction goes back to Roman Law."

To declare War, grant Letters of Marque and Reprisal, and make Rules concerning Captures on Land and Water;

32

Only Congress can declare war. That's why we haven't gone to "war" since the 1940s.; the prevailing thought being that if you don't call it war you don't need permission from Congress. Letters of marque and reprisal are, in effect, granted permissions to take action outside of the United States for private retribution. Marque means border and reprisal means retaliation. Congress may authorize private action against foreign entities. This is not the same as declaring war, which is state military action, though letters came to be used to allow action against non-states as well. In both cases, state and private, as authorized, Congress sets the rules regarding those captured on land and water.

To raise and support Armies, but no Appropriation of Money to that Use shall be for a longer Term than two Years;

Congress can raise and support Armies, but appropriations made for such use can only be for two years or less. Every two years there is an option to not raise and support an Army.

To provide and maintain a Navy;

Unlike the Army, permission to provide for a Navy is granted in perpetuity. Until air travel, the nation's ocean borders were the primary concern, as invasion by sea was the only method, and a Navy was required at all times to protect them.

To make Rules for the Government and Regulation of the land and naval Forces;

Congress also sets the rules, both governing and directing, of the land and naval forces, the Armies and Navy.

To provide for calling forth the Militia to execute the Laws of the Union, suppress Insurrections and repel Invasions;

Unlike state Armies, the Militia is ordinary citizens called up for military service at specific times. Congress may call forth the Militia to execute laws of the Union, suppress insurrections and repel invasions. This is done to keep from having a professional military police the people. Notice that is says Congress can provide for calling for the Militia.

Congress has authority to request the Militia, but no Militia is required to respond to the call.

To provide for organizing, arming, and disciplining, the Militia, and for governing such Part of them as may be employed in the Service of the United States, reserving to the States respectively, the Appointment of the Officers, and the Authority of training the Militia according to the discipline prescribed by Congress;

Once the Militia heeds the call, Congress is authorized to organize, arm and discipline the militia. Congress is further authorized to govern the Militia when in service of the United States, but the States are reserved the appointment of officers and the actual training according to the discipline prescribed by Congress. Congress sets the framework, but the States manage the specifics.

To exercise exclusive Legislation in all Cases whatsoever, over such District (not exceeding ten Miles square) as may, by Cession of particular States, and the Acceptance of Congress, become the Seat of the Government of the United States, and to exercise like Authority over all Places purchased by the Consent of the Legislature of the State in which the Same shall be, for the Erection of Forts, Magazines, Arsenals, dock-Yards, and other needful Buildings;--And

Congress has exclusive legislation over any district, not to exceed ten square miles, as ceded by particular States, and accepted by Congress, that is the Seat of the Government of the United States. The City of Washington has existed since 1790. Congress first met there officially as the Seat in 1800. It officially became the District of Columbia, its formal name, in 1871. Congress then has like authority over all places purchased by it from a State by consent of its State Legislature, primarily for specific military uses, but also other needful buildings.

To make all Laws which shall be necessary and proper for carrying into Execution the foregoing Powers, and all other Powers vested by this Constitution in the Government of the United States, or in any Department or Officer thereof.

Congress has authority to make all laws deemed necessary and proper for carrying out the powers given to it above and all powers granted by this

34

Constitution to the Government of the United States or any Department or Officer thereof. It is one great check on Congressional authority. The Constitution creates the government, its Departments and Officers. It assigns specific powers to that Government, its Departments and its Officers. Each is limited by the exact allowance given to it by the Constitution. From there, Congress has authority to make all laws necessary and proper for executing those powers. In short, if the power is not found in the Constitution as belonging to the Government of the United States, its Departments or its Officers, Congress does not have authority to make laws regarding it. If someone wishes to add a power and add laws, they need to amend the Constitution.

Section. 9.

The Migration or Importation of such Persons as any of the States now existing shall think proper to admit, shall not be prohibited by the Congress prior to the Year one thousand eight hundred and eight, but a Tax or duty may be imposed on such Importation, not exceeding ten dollars for each Person.

Congress may not prohibit the migration of importation of any Persons to any State until 1808, but it may impose a tax or duty on the importation of Persons so long as it does not exceed ten dollars for each Person. Without blatantly spelling it out, this was the acknowledgment of slavery and giving States a stay on it until at least 1808.

The Privilege of the Writ of Habeas Corpus shall not be suspended, unless when in Cases of Rebellion or Invasion the public Safety may require it.

The Privilege of the Writ of Habeas Corpus, from the Latin, meaning "You shall have the body," is a legal privilege to guarantee a person must be taken to court and sentenced for imprisonment rather than being arrested and detained indefinitely. It is to prevent abuse by the judicial system. It can be suspended, but only when the public safety requires it in cases of rebellion or invasion. Abraham Lincoln suspended Habeas Corpus in the 1860s. Ulysses S. Grant suspended it in the 1870s. Through the Military Commissions Act of 2006, it was again suspended by George W. Bush, but the Supreme Court of the United States found the Act unconstitutional in 2008.

No Bill of Attainder or ex post facto Law shall be passed.

Congress is not permitted to pass a Bill of Attainder, a bill whereby a person or persons are declared guilty without a trial, nor any ex post facto law, a law which retroactively takes effect at a time before it is passed, such as punishing for actions made before the law declared them illegal.

No Capitation, or other direct, Tax shall be laid, unless in Proportion to the Census or enumeration herein before directed to be taken.

No capitation, a tax levied per head, per person, nor any other direct tax, shall be laid unless it is in proportion to the census. Taxes levied to States must be in equal proportion based on population and taxes levied to individuals must likewise be equal per person. Direct taxes are levied directly to the taxpayer with no intermediary, as opposed to indirect taxes which are simply passed along in the price of the goods they are added to and paid for by the final purchase of the good. If you sell anything, the cost of any tax you pay can be passed along to someone else in the price of the good you sell, provided there is still a buyer for it.

No Tax or Duty shall be laid on Articles exported from any State.

Taxes or duties may not be added to anything exported from any State, this includes interstate commerce as those goods are exported from State A and imported into State B. It's not just about exports to foreign nations. States are sovereign political entities.

No Preference shall be given by any Regulation of Commerce or Revenue to the Ports of one State over those of another; nor shall Vessels bound to, or from, one State, be obliged to enter, clear, or pay Duties in another.

All trade of any kind is to be treated equally and no preference, good or bad, is to be given to any port from any State. Also, no vessel may be required to enter, clear or pay duties in another State. Ports are points of entry for goods and persons. Vessels are carriers of those goods and persons.

No Money shall be drawn from the Treasury, but in Consequence of Appropriations made by Law; and a regular Statement and Account of the Receipts and Expenditures of all public Money shall be published from time to time.

No money shall be drawn from the Treasury unless it is for appropriations made by law. The Congress is prohibited from spending money it does not appropriate by legislation. Also, a regular statement and account of the receipts and expenditures of all public money shall be published from time to time, meaning they are required to open up the books and show what was paid where, why and to whom.

No Title of Nobility shall be granted by the United States: And no Person holding any Office of Profit or Trust under them, shall, without the Consent of the Congress, accept of any present, Emolument, Office, or Title, of any kind whatever, from any King, Prince, or foreign State.

The United States grants no titles of nobility. There will be no class separation by title, such as Lord, Duke, etc. No person holding any Office of profit or trust, elected, appointed or hired, shall accept any gift, payment, office or title of any kind, from any king, prince or foreign State without the consent of the Congress. No officer of the United States is allowed to receive anything from any foreign leader or State unless Congress agrees to it.

Section. 10.

No State shall enter into any Treaty, Alliance, or Confederation; grant Letters of Marque and Reprisal; coin Money; emit Bills of Credit; make any Thing but gold and silver Coin a Tender in Payment of Debts; pass any Bill of Attainder, ex post facto Law, or Law impairing the Obligation of Contracts, or grant any Title of Nobility.

No State in the United States shall enter into any treaty, alliance or confederation. On these matters the United States are together as one through the federal government. States are outright forbidden from granting letters of marque and reprisal, coining money or issuing credit. The United States may issue credit, but Virginia and Connecticut may not. States may not allow anything other than gold and silver as legal tender in payment of debts. Like the Congress, States also may not pass any bill of attainder or ex post facto law or grant any title of nobility. States are also forbidden from passing laws which impair the obligation of contracts. They may not pass laws to relieve anyone from their contractual obligations.

No State shall, without the Consent of the Congress, lay any Imposts or Duties on Imports or Exports, except what may be absolutely necessary for executing it's [sic] *inspection Laws: and the net Produce of all Duties and Imposts, laid by any State on Imports or Exports, shall be for the Use of the Treasury of the United States; and all such Laws shall be subject to the Revision and Controul of the Congress.*

No State can charge imposts or duties on any imports or exports without permission from Congress except as shall be absolutely necessary for executing its inspection laws. States need to make sure their detailed inspection costs match up with any duties or imposts they charge. Anything more must be approved by Congress. However, the net gain of all duties or imposts, any charges beyond covering actual costs, goes to the Treasury of the United States, meaning States cannot gain revenue at all from them. On top of this, all impost and duty laws are subject to the revision and control of Congress, so Congress can attach any imposts or duties the Constitution allows and the States must comply with them, yet never earn revenue from them, just do the work on behalf of the United States. States can pass such laws, but must prove to Congress they cover actual costs, or else Congress must approve the laws, so, either way, Congress approves all such laws and can change them at any time.

No State shall, without the Consent of Congress, lay any Duty of Tonnage, keep Troops, or Ships of War in time of Peace, enter into any Agreement or Compact with another State, or with a foreign Power, or engage in War, unless actually invaded, or in such imminent Danger as will not admit of delay.

States require Congressional consent to: attach duties based on weight; to keep any troops or ships of war in time of peace; to enter into any sort of agreement or compact with another State or foreign power; to engage in war unless actually invaded or in such imminent danger that no delay is allowable.

Article II

Section. 1.

The executive Power shall be vested in a President of the United States of America. He shall hold his Office during the Term of four Years, and, together with the Vice President, chosen for the same Term, be elected, as follows:

The executive power is given to the President of the United States of America. He and the Vice President shall serve together for terms of four years and be chosen as follows:

Each State shall appoint, in such Manner as the Legislature thereof may direct, a Number of Electors, equal to the whole Number of Senators and Representatives to which the State may be entitled in the Congress: but no Senator or Representative, or Person holding an Office of Trust or Profit under the United States, shall be appointed an Elector.

Each State shall, in a way chosen and directed by the Legislature, appoint Electors in a number equal to the whole of Senators and Representatives that State is entitled in Congress. No Senator, Representative, or other person holding an Office of trust or profit under the United States shall be appointed as an Elector. No person may in any way work for the Government of the United States and be an Elector.

The Electors shall meet in their respective States, and vote by Ballot for two Persons, of whom one at least shall not be an Inhabitant of the same State with themselves. And they shall make a List of all the Persons voted for, and of the Number of Votes for each; which List they shall sign and certify, and transmit sealed to the Seat of the Government of the United States, directed to the President of the Senate. The President of the Senate shall, in the Presence of the Senate and House of Representatives, open all the Certificates, and the Votes shall then be counted. The Person having the greatest Number of Votes shall be the President, if such Number be a Majority of the whole Number of Electors appointed; and if there be more than one who have such Majority, and have an equal Number of Votes, then the House of

Representatives shall immediately chuse by Ballot one of them for President; and if no Person have a Majority, then from the five highest on the List the said House shall in like Manner chuse the President. But in chusing the President, the Votes shall be taken by States, the Representation from each State having one Vote; A quorum for this purpose shall consist of a Member or Members from two thirds of the States, and a Majority of all the States shall be necessary to a Choice. In every Case, after the Choice of the President, the Person having the greatest Number of Votes of the Electors shall be the Vice President. But if there should remain two or more who have equal Votes, the Senate shall chuse from them by Ballot the Vice President.

The Electors shall meet in their own States and vote by ballot for two persons, of whom at least one shall not be an inhabitant of their same State. They shall make a list of all persons voted for and the number of votes for each. The list is then signed, certified, sealed and sent to the Seat of Government of the United States, directed to the President of the Senate.

The President of the Senate shall, in the presence of the Senate and House of Representatives, open all the certificates and the votes shall then be counted. The person having the most votes, if that number is also a majority of the whole of Electors appointed, is President. If more than one person has the same count, also being a majority, the President shall immediately be chosen, from those tied, by ballot by the House of Representatives.

If, however, there is no person with a majority, the House shall choose the President, but shall do so in a different manner. The top five vote recipients shall go on a list. The House shall vote by State with one vote for each State, each delegation deciding amongst themselves how their vote will be cast. For this process, quorum shall be having at least one member present from at least two thirds of the States and the chosen President needs a majority of States. So, with 50 states currently, there need to be Electors from at least 34 States present. A majority is half plus one, so 18 States are needed to become President.

Once the President is chosen, in whichever manner is necessary, the next highest vote recipient shall be the Vice President. However, if there is a tie for Vice President in this way, the Senate shall choose by ballot, from among those tied, the Vice President. No mention is made of breaking a tie in this Senate vote, so it is left to refer to the earlier section whereby the sitting Vice President has the final vote on the next Vice President.

This whole process may seem rather obtuse, but it is really quite calculated. This was not merely a matter of travel and communication difficulties at the time, but also a long term protection against mob rule. Absolute power in an unchecked majority can be just as dangerous as absolute power in an individual. The Congress is structured so that each State has its own safeguard in the Senate, the people have theirs in the direct choosing of the House, and the House and Senate check against each other. This was done on purpose to keep power divided. It's one thing for a State to have direct election of statewide offices. Each State can do it differently and it is unlikely that all States will follow the same manner. People have the freedom to leave one State and go to another. However, a direct, national election, choosing any office by national popular vote, especially the President, is the very epitome of the tyranny by majority the framers sought to avoid. There is no promise that any majority of people will always make the best decision, that they are not easily swayed or misled in some way. All other elections have checks and counterbalances to minimize the power afforded to any one person or State if that should happen. A national, popular vote for President has no such check. The entire office of the President would rise or fall by the opinion of the majority.

It is not enough to say the power of the office is checked by the Congress or the Judiciary. The Electoral College provides a buffer between the highest office in the land and a mob mentality. Moreover, it is yet another recognition of State sovereignty. The States come together to form the United States. Likewise, the States, not the people, come together in choosing the President. The people have their say within their States. They choose their own Legislature, who sets the means for choosing Electors, which may even allow for direct selection of Electors by the people. In this way, the people are not removed from choosing the President, but are not wholly entrusted with it either.

This is another greatly misconstrued idea in modern politics. Specifically, it is party politics which ruins the integrity of elections themselves, much less the choosing of Electors for choosing a President. Apart from constitutional limits and provisions, the party holding a legislative majority, and possibly executive power, sets the rules for election in a State whatsoever. Most, if not all, States choose Electors through party politics. The people will vote for a candidate ticket, saying "I want Person A for President and Person B for Vice President," but what actually happens is they are saying "I like the candidates of Party A and I trust Party A and the slate of Electors they have lined up, even though I have no idea who they are." Unless State election law says otherwise, parties choose their Electors internally and the party receiving the majority of a State's popular vote (though, often times, a simple plurality lead is allowed), automatically has its entire slate of Electors as that State's delegation to the Electoral College (a term not actually found within this Constitution). The perceived problem is not with the electoral system as prescribed here, but with the specific choosing of Electors within States.

There is a great difference between believing campaign rhetoric, listening to abstract ideas and advertisements, or even just lining up with a party regardless of candidates, and having Electors at your local level who can tell you what they believe and what they offer in choosing the President. The voter has a better chance to know and test his local candidates for Elector than he does a national figure that spends months going from State to State raising money and giving speeches. The closer your government is to you, the more say you have in it. Despite its appearance, a national, popular vote for anyone or anything is the antithesis of keeping government close to the people.

The Congress may determine the Time of chusing the Electors, and the Day on which they shall give their Votes; which Day shall be the same throughout the United States.

Congress may determine the time of choosing the Electors. It does not say must or shall, but may, so Congress may leave this up to the States to decide, or States can refuse to comply with any date set by Congress. States already decide how Electors are chosen and Congress has no control over that. Congress may likewise choose the day on which the Electors vote. If they do so, that day is meant to be the same throughout all the United States, so long as all States abide by it. Again, it does not say that it must be done in this way, that Congress must determine when the Electors vote, only that it may. Arguably, Congress can set a date for Electors to vote and a single State could refuse to comply. Congress does not have absolute power in this. For all the States which comply, their Electors vote on the same day, but any State choosing to handle their own affairs may do so according to their own terms.

No Person except a natural born Citizen, or a Citizen of the United States, at the time of the Adoption of this Constitution, shall be eligible to the Office of President; neither shall any Person be eligible to that Office who shall not have attained to the Age of thirty five Years, and been fourteen Years a Resident within the United States.

A person must be a natural born citizen of the United States, of one of the States, or such citizen at the time of the adoption of the Constitution, to be President. Seeing as the Constitution was adopted in 1787, it has been a long time since anyone could qualify without being a natural born citizen. This was set intentionally to prevent foreign influence from the office of the President. Without this control, someone could live for decades elsewhere, come to the United States, become a citizen, and become President. The assumption is that persons who are citizens of any foreign State prior to becoming citizens of the United States are too open to divided allegiances and foreign influence and no such person should hold the highest office in the United States.

Moreover, a person must also be at least thirty five years of age and been a resident within the United States for fourteen years. This second part may have applied more at the start, whereby it disqualified anyone who had been a resident for less than fourteen years at the time of adoption in 1787, at least until they reach those fourteen years. Currently, however, residency is determined by laws in the United States Code, so, any person who meets the other criteria and has spent fourteen years as a resident within the United States is eligible. It does not say the fourteen years must be consecutive, nor concurrent with nomination or election. If it is permissible by law for someone to be a citizen while not being a resident and they have previously been a resident for fourteen years, they meet this requirement. It is what is written in the Constitution. To specify the residency must be consecutive and concurrent with nomination or election for the Presidency requires no less than amending the Constitution.

In Case of the Removal of the President from Office, or of his Death, Resignation, or Inability to discharge the Powers and Duties of the said

Office, the Same shall devolve on the Vice President, and the Congress may by Law provide for the Case of Removal, Death, Resignation or Inability, both of the President and Vice President, declaring what Officer shall then act as President, and such Officer shall act accordingly, until the Disability be removed, or a President shall be elected.

If the President dies, resigns, is removed or otherwise unable to discharge the Powers and Duties of the Presidency, the Vice President assumes those Powers and Duties. It says the Powers and Duties are assumed, but it does not say the Vice President does, in fact, become President in name or title. Furthermore, in case of the removal, death, resignation or inability of both the President and Vice President, the Congress, through law, may declare which Officer shall then act as President until the disability is removed or a President is elected. In other words, Congress can say who comes next after the Vice President to hold the Powers and Duties, but not the Office, of the President.

The President shall, at stated Times, receive for his Services, a Compensation, which shall neither be increased nor diminished during the Period for which he shall have been elected, and he shall not receive within that Period any other Emolument from the United States, or any of them.

The President shall be compensated for his services, but that compensation shall not be changed during the term for which he was elected. Any change to the President's compensation takes effect after the next Presidential election and no sooner. Also, the President is not allowed, while in office, to be additionally compensated in any way by the United States or any of the States themselves.

Before he enter on the Execution of his Office, he shall take the following Oath or Affirmation:--"I do solemnly swear (or affirm) that I will faithfully execute the Office of President of the United States, and will to the best of my Ability, preserve, protect and defend the Constitution of the United States."

Before beginning to execute the Office of President, he must take this oath, whereby he swears (or affirms) to execute the Office of President of the United States and, more importantly, to the best of his ability,

44

preserve, protect and defend the Constitution of the United States. That means following it, unless one admits that the best of his ability falls short of being able to do so. You cannot preserve, protect or defend any rule or standard of law without abiding by it.

Section. 2.

The President shall be Commander in Chief of the Army and Navy of the United States, and of the Militia of the several States, when called into the actual Service of the United States; he may require the Opinion, in writing, of the principal Officer in each of the executive Departments, upon any Subject relating to the Duties of their respective Offices, and he shall have Power to grant Reprieves and Pardons for Offences against the United States, except in Cases of Impeachment.

The President is Commander in Chief of the Army and Navy of the United States at all times and of the State Militias when they are called into service of the United States. At any time he may require that each principal Officer of each executive department submit to him, in writing, an opinion pertaining to a subject relating to the duties of their respective Offices. Principal Officers, Department Secretaries or otherwise, of each executive Department, are required to respond to the President when he requests their opinion on matters of their Offices. The President also has power to grant reprieves, temporary relief, and pardons, permanent relief, for Offenses against the United States, except in cases of impeachment.

He shall have Power, by and with the Advice and Consent of the Senate, to make Treaties, provided two thirds of the Senators present concur; and he shall nominate, and by and with the Advice and Consent of the Senate, shall appoint Ambassadors, other public Ministers and Consuls, Judges of the supreme Court, and all other Officers of the United States, whose Appointments are not herein otherwise provided for, and which shall be established by Law: but the Congress may by Law vest the Appointment of such inferior Officers, as they think proper, in the President alone, in the Courts of Law, or in the Heads of Departments.

The President has power to make treaties, but the Senate is to advise and consent to them, as they represent the States themselves, and two thirds of the Senators present, but not of the whole Senate, must concur. The Senate is also to advise and consent on the President's appointments as Ambassadors, other public ministers and consuls, Judges of the supreme Court and all other Officers of the United States whose appointments are not otherwise provided for in this Constitution, including those later established by law. However, unlike with treaties, the Senate must only give their consent to the appointments. It is not required to have two thirds concur on them. The Senate may set its own standard for what it means to consent, it is just not required by the Constitution to be two thirds of the Senators present. The Congress is also authorized to make law allowing the President, the courts and department heads to appoint inferior officers, those for whom the Constitution does not otherwise set specific requirements for their appointments, without any consent by the Senate. Ultimately, the Senate must consent to all appointments unless it removes itself from those appointments below those specifically stated in the Constitution.

The President shall have Power to fill up all Vacancies that may happen during the Recess of the Senate, by granting Commissions which shall expire at the End of their next Session.

The President has power to fill all vacancies that may happen during the recess of the Senate, regardless of the required procedure for their appointment, by granting Commissions. Such recess appointments, as they have been called, expire at the end of the next session of the Senate.

Section. 3.

He shall from time to time give to the Congress Information of the State of the Union, and recommend to their Consideration such Measures as he shall judge necessary and expedient; he may, on extraordinary Occasions, convene both Houses, or either of them, and in Case of Disagreement between them, with Respect to the Time of Adjournment, he may adjourn them to such Time as he shall think proper; he shall receive Ambassadors and other public Ministers; he shall take Care that the Laws be faithfully executed, and shall Commission all the Officers of the United States.

As the full-time head of the government, the President shall, from time to time, give to the Congress information on the State of the Union, the political body of the Union of the United States and the affairs delegated to this government, not the condition of a singular geographic entity called The United States, and make recommendations for their consideration such measures as he may judge to be necessary and expedient. Remember, the Congress writes the laws, but it is up to the President to be in charge of executing and administering the laws. He oversees the government which carries out the laws written by Congress. This is the CEO reporting to the Board of Directors to make recommendations about things to address or change, but the Board, the Congress, is still limited by this Constitution. There is nothing requiring the President to address both Houses at once much less in person or at any given time of the year.

The President may also, on extraordinary occasions, though not solely tied to giving the information described above, convene either or both Houses of Congress since they're not in session throughout the whole year. If the Houses disagree on a time of adjournment in this case, he may adjourn them to such time as he thinks proper. The President shall also receive ambassadors and other public ministers. He shall also take care that the laws are faithfully executed and shall Commission all Officers of the United States.

Section. 4.

The President, Vice President and all civil Officers of the United States, shall be removed from Office on Impeachment for, and Conviction of, Treason, Bribery, or other high Crimes and Misdemeanors.

The President, Vice President and all civil Officers of the United States shall be removed from Office after having been impeached for and convicted of treason, bribery or other high crimes and misdemeanors. "High crimes and misdemeanors" means "high crimes" and "high misdemeanors." Treason and bribery are but two examples of them. High is not a condition of the offense, but of the person committing the crime. A person holding high Office, such as the President, Vice President or other Officers, can be impeached and removed from Office for crimes and misdemeanors. Any crime or misdemeanor is a breach of trust of their Offices.

Article III

Section. 1.

The judicial Power of the United States shall be vested in one supreme Court, and in such inferior Courts as the Congress may from time to time ordain and establish. The Judges, both of the supreme and inferior Courts, shall hold their Offices during good Behaviour, and shall, at stated Times, receive for their Services a Compensation, which shall not be diminished during their Continuance in Office.

The judicial power of the United States is given to the supreme Court (note that it is not titled as supreme, just designated as being such) and all such inferior Courts as the Congress may ordain and establish. This is not all judicial power outright, just that in the government of the United States. Each State can establish its own internal judicial authority as it sees fit. Judges of these United States courts shall hold their Offices during good behaviour. It is not stated that judges sit for life, but they are not specifically held to any specific duration of time like the President, Vice President or members of Congress. They may be impeached or resign from office, otherwise they serve throughout their lives. These judges, like other Officers of the United States, shall be compensated. Their compensation shall never diminish during their time in Office.

Section. 2.

The judicial Power shall extend to all Cases, in Law and Equity, arising under this Constitution, the Laws of the United States, and Treaties made, or which shall be made, under their Authority;--to all Cases affecting Ambassadors, other public Ministers and Consuls;--to all Cases of admiralty and maritime Jurisdiction;--to Controversies to which the United States shall be a Party;--to Controversies between two or more States;-- between a State and Citizens of another State,-- between Citizens of different States,--between Citizens of the same State claiming Lands under Grants of different States, and between a State, or the Citizens thereof, and foreign States, Citizens or Subjects.

48

This judicial power extends to all cases, in law and equity, written and common law, which arise under this Constitution, the laws of the United States and any treaties which are or shall be made under the authority of the Constitution or laws of the United States. This judicial power also extends to: all cases affecting Ambassadors and other public Ministers and Consuls; all cases of admiralty (the navy) and maritime jurisdiction (matters at sea); controversies to which the United States itself is party; controversies between States, between a State and a citizen of another State, between citizens of different States, between citizens of the same State claiming lands under the authority of different States and between a State, or the citizens thereof, and any foreign States, citizens or subjects. In short, the courts of the United States have judicial power over matters of the government of the United States, including where the United States itself is a party to the case, naval and maritime matters, and any State or citizen matters which in any way involve other States, foreign or domestic. State courts have the power over all internal cases not involving other States or the United States itself.

In all Cases affecting Ambassadors, other public Ministers and Consuls, and those in which a State shall be Party, the supreme Court shall have original Jurisdiction. In all the other Cases before mentioned, the supreme Court shall have appellate Jurisdiction, both as to Law and Fact, with such Exceptions, and under such Regulations as the Congress shall make.

The supreme court has original jurisdiction over all cases involving Ambassadors, other public Ministers and Consuls, and any case in which a State shall be party. In all other cases previously mentioned, they being naval and maritime matters as well as cases where the United States is party or a particular State is involved but not party, the supreme Court has appellate jurisdiction, to both law and fact, the law itself and the facts pertaining to its application, rather than just facts as applied to the law, with such exceptions and under such regulations as the Congress shall make. This means the supreme Court is the appellate court and can rule over laws in certain cases, not just their facts, but that the Congress can make laws restricting that ability. Congress cannot, however, make such exceptions to the cases of its original jurisdiction, i.e. Ambassadors et al. and where a State is party to the case.

The Trial of all Crimes, except in Cases of Impeachment, shall be by Jury; and such Trial shall be held in the State where the said Crimes shall have been committed; but when not committed within any State, the Trial shall be at such Place or Places as the Congress may by Law have directed.

All criminal trials, except in cases of Impeachment, shall be trials by jury and are to be held in the State where the crimes have been committed. If not committed within any State, the trial shall be at such place or places as the Congress may, by law, direct. Note that is says the trial of all crimes. It does not designate specifically crimes falling under the previously named jurisdiction of the United States. If it came to it, this can be cited to prevent a crime wholly committed and pertaining to only one State from being tried, for whatever reason, in another State.

Section. 3.

Treason against the United States, shall consist only in levying War against them, or in adhering to their Enemies, giving them Aid and Comfort. No Person shall be convicted of Treason unless on the Testimony of two Witnesses to the same overt Act, or on Confession in open Court.

Treason against the United States shall only be defined as levying war against them (not it, but them) or in adhering to their enemies, giving them aid and comfort. Treason is levying war against the United States or giving aid and comfort to their enemies. To be convicted of treason requires the testimony of two witnesses to the same overt act or on confession to the crime in open Court.

The Congress shall have Power to declare the Punishment of Treason, but no Attainder of Treason shall work Corruption of Blood, or Forfeiture except during the Life of the Person attainted.

The Congress has power to declare the punishment for treason. However, no punishment for treason shall carry the loss of property or title beyond the life of the person condemned. If a person is found guilty of treason and stripped of property or title, such punishment does not carry forward beyond anyone but the convicted. His descendants cannot be punished for his crime.

Article IV

Section. 1.

Full Faith and Credit shall be given in each State to the public Acts, Records, and judicial Proceedings of every other State. And the Congress may by general Laws prescribe the Manner in which such Acts, Records and Proceedings shall be proved, and the Effect thereof.

Each State shall give full faith and credit to the public acts, records and judicial proceedings of every other State. This means that States shall recognize the licenses, judgments and other official records of other States. Alone it is a statement of absolution, that all legal documents originating in one State must be recognized in any other. Its predecessor in the Articles of Confederation was more direct and limited, specifying the acts, records and judicial proceedings to be from courts and magistrates. It meant courts in one State were to recognize the actions of courts in another State. It said nothing of legislative or executive authorizations. The intent, it seemed, was to keep people within the United States from trying to escape legal obligations by fleeing to other States. As written, this Constitutional provision is not as pointed, but stated more broadly so as to authorize the general enforcement.

The second sentence, however, gives Congress oversight to declare by law the manner in which these acts, records and judicial proceedings shall be proved and the effect they shall have. In short, the first sentence declares full faith and credit be given to anything, but the second sentence truncates that by allowing Congress to set parameters. Congress can say which sorts of acts, records and judicial proceedings shall be recognized in full. So, the Constitution declares the power to enforce from State to State but the Congress can set the specifics on which things are to be enforced and how.

Generally, this provision has been taken to mean that a person holding specific legal recognitions, such as marriage licenses, will not have to re-apply for the same recognition in each State, the intent being that if two States have the same provision, a person only needs to be recognized in one to be recognized in the other. However, such applications are dependent wholly upon Acts of Congress.

Section. 2.

The Citizens of each State shall be entitled to all Privileges and Immunities of Citizens in the several States.

No citizen of any State will be treated any differently, in regard to privileges and immunities, while in another State, than the citizens of that State which they are in. Virginia cannot pass laws to treat people from Maryland any differently than they treat Virginians.

A Person charged in any State with Treason, Felony, or other Crime, who shall flee from Justice, and be found in another State, shall on Demand of the executive Authority of the State from which he fled, be delivered up, to be removed to the State having Jurisdiction of the Crime.

A person charged with crimes, should he flee to another State to escape justice, shall be, on demand of the executive Authority of the State from which he fled, delivered up and returned to the State having jurisdiction of the crime.

No Person held to Service or Labour in one State, under the Laws thereof, escaping into another, shall, in Consequence of any Law or Regulation therein, be discharged from such Service or Labour, but shall be delivered up on Claim of the Party to whom such Service or Labour may be due.

No person bound to service or labor in one State may flee to immunity in another State, regardless of the laws therein. Such persons are obligated, on claim of the party to whom service or labor is due, to be returned to the State and claimant to which they are legally bound.

Section. 3.

New States may be admitted by the Congress into this Union; but no new State shall be formed or erected within the Jurisdiction of any other State; nor any State be formed by the Junction of two or more States, or Parts of States, without the Consent of the Legislatures of the States concerned as well as of the Congress.

Congress is allowed to approve and admit new States into this Union, the United States, but any State formed within an existing State, or by joining two or more States, or parts of States, requires the consent of the Legislatures of those States involved as well as the Congress. What we know as Maine originally belonged to Massachusetts. Maine could not be approved for statehood by Congress without the consent of the Massachusetts Legislature.

The Congress shall have Power to dispose of and make all needful Rules and Regulations respecting the Territory or other Property belonging to the United States; and nothing in this Constitution shall be so construed as to Prejudice any Claims of the United States, or of any particular State.

The Congress has authority to deal with and make necessary rules and regulations for all Territory or other property belonging to the United States. Nothing in this Constitution shall be construed as giving prejudice or any other preference to the claims of the United States or any particular State. Each claim to land will be decided by its own merit. Congress is only given authority to those properties recognized as belonging to the United States, not any right of claim to land not so recognized. This lack of preference for Congress is not to be taken as preference to any individual State.

Section. 4.

The United States shall guarantee to every State in this Union a Republican Form of Government, and shall protect each of them against Invasion; and on Application of the Legislature, or of the Executive (when the Legislature cannot be convened), against domestic Violence.

The United States guarantees to every State a Republican form of government, which is to say a Republic. Further, the United States shall protect each of them from Invasion as well as domestic violence, but the latter only when requested by the State Legislature or, when the Legislature cannot be convened, by the Executive of that State.

The second part is straightforward. The United States is to protect all States from invasion and, when asked, against domestic violence. It is the first part which seems to get overlooked or misunderstood on occasion. The States are guaranteed a Republican form of government. The Constitution could have just as easily guaranteed a Democratic form of government, but it did not.

A Republic is a nation of law. Not all republics are presidential. Not all republics are constitutional. The word republic comes from Latin and means "public thing." The core of a republic is a thing, a central public law. This is not the same as Democracy. Democracy is from Greek and means "rule or strength of the people." Democracy is pure majority rule.

The difference could not be clearer. A Republic puts some measure of limitations on the power of government while a Democracy grants absolute authority to the will of the people. A Republic is limited by established law. In the case of the United States, this law stems from the recognition of individual rights and sovereignty and serves to protect those rights. A Democracy is simply rule by majority will.

A common description of the case of rule by majority is that of two wolves and a lamb voting on what to have for dinner, the obvious point being that the lamb has no protection from the will of the majority to deprive it of its rights, in this case its life. A slightly more elaborate take may put it this way:

Say you live on a street with nine neighbors, ten people in total. You and eight other people work hard for a living, the tenth person does not. By consequence or fortune, you own two cars while your eight working neighbors each have one. The ninth neighbor, of course, has none. Should you give your other car to him? You could. You own the car and can do with it as you wish, including giving it to someone else. That is your choice. Suppose you don't want to. Suppose your neighbors think that you should. In a Democracy, your nine neighbors can hold a vote on whether or not to give your car to the one. Even if you have three neighbors agreeing with you, you are still outvoted six to four. By will of the majority, your neighbors take your car and give it to your non-working neighbor. More likely than not, this would be done in the names of "fairness" and "equality."

Sure, sometimes you may be in the majority, but that does not entitle you to take from others. Taking by will of the majority is asserting that your right to choice is somehow superior to their right to property. Elections are different. Voting is a privilege concurrent and commensurate with citizenship. There is no right to choose for others. Doing so goes against their own inherent claim to a right of a choice. There is no right to a choice which directly diminishes the rights of others. There can, however, be an allowance of a choice, if deemed by law, in which participants have an equal say in the choosing toward a cumulative outcome. This is a granted privilege, not a right. Electing a person to a position in government does not mean an automatic and direct consequence to your rights or the rights of any minority group. Elections are simply voicing a preference in representation. By voting you exercise your equal privilege of opportunity just as others do. Legal resident aliens have the same protection of rights as full citizens but are not afforded the privilege of a vote. Legitimacy of the vote is not found in the action of voting but in what the vote is over. Not all things, in fact, very few, can be decided by a vote of the majority without direct consequence on the rights of all, thus voting is not an inherent right of choice.

To leave the United States to Democracy is to leave them to constant arguments and struggles for absolute supremacy. People split into factions and fight for control over others. It's self-evident. The more you push for Democracy, the more you attack a structure of laws and rights and devolve into chaos with tyranny not far behind.

Article V

The Congress, whenever two thirds of both Houses shall deem it necessary, shall propose Amendments to this Constitution, or, on the Application of the Legislatures of two thirds of the several States, shall call a Convention for proposing Amendments, which, in either Case, shall be valid to all Intents and Purposes, as Part of this Constitution, when ratified by the Legislatures of three fourths of the several States, or by Conventions in three fourths thereof, as the one or the other Mode of Ratification may be proposed by the Congress; Provided that no Amendment which may be made prior to the Year One thousand eight hundred and eight shall in any Manner affect the first and fourth Clauses in the Ninth Section of the first Article; and that no State, without its Consent, shall be deprived of its equal Suffrage in the Senate.

The Congress shall either propose Amendments to this Constitution when two thirds of both Houses agree it is necessary, or call a Convention for proposing Amendments when the Legislatures of two thirds of the States act on Congress to do so.

In either case, the Amendments shall be valid to all intents and purposes, as part of this Constitution, when they have been ratified by the Legislatures of three fourths of the States or by Conventions in three fourths of the States. Congress may propose either mode of ratification.

There are two exceptions to the Amendment process. No Amendment made prior to 1808 shall affect Article I, Section 9, Clauses 1 or 4. No State shall be deprived of its equal suffrage in the Senate. The first cannot be touched by Amendment until 1808 and the second cannot be amended at all.

Article VI

All Debts contracted and Engagements entered into, before the Adoption of this Constitution, shall be as valid against the United States under this Constitution, as under the Confederation.

All debts contracted and financial obligations entered into under the Confederation shall be just as valid against the United States under this Constitution as before its adoption.

This Constitution, and the Laws of the United States which shall be made in Pursuance thereof; and all Treaties made, or which shall be made, under the Authority of the United States, shall be the supreme Law of the Land; and the Judges in every State shall be bound thereby, any Thing in the Constitution or Laws of any State to the Contrary notwithstanding.

This Constitution, the laws of the United States made to carry it out, and all treaties made, or which shall be made, under the authority of the United States, shall be the supreme law of the land. Judges in every State shall be bound to them regardless of the State Constitution or laws. This Constitution, its constitutional laws, and all treaties, supersede any State laws.

The Senators and Representatives before mentioned, and the Members of the several State Legislatures, and all executive and judicial Officers, both of the United States and of the several States, shall be bound by Oath or Affirmation, to support this Constitution; but no religious Test shall ever be required as a Qualification to any Office or public Trust under the United States.

Similar to the Article II, Section 1, Clause 8, regarding the President, all Senators, Representatives, members of State Legislatures and executive and judicial Officers, both of the United States and the States, shall be bound by oath or affirmation to this Constitution.

No religious test shall ever be required as a qualification for any Office or public Trust subject to the authority, direction or supervision of the United States. This does not bar laws establishing or requiring religious tests. This bars all religious tests. It sets a standard saying that religion shall not be a factor in holding office. Rather than being a directive about writing laws, it is law. Unfortunately, it only has real effect if argued in court against the claim that someone did set some religious test for fitness of Office.

As people bring their social, moral and religious standards to bear on the electoral process, they are, in effect, setting religious tests, person by person, or through organizations, to support or denounce candidates for Office based on religious views. No candidate for Office should ever be questioned or judged by their religious views. No religious beliefs should enter law or elections whatsoever. You may judge their private character and their public actions in fitness for Office, but never their religious beliefs or lack thereof. If you say someone should or should not hold office simply because they are or are not of some religious belief, sect or denomination, you are violating the Constitution.

Article VII

The Ratification of the Conventions of nine States, shall be sufficient for the Establishment of this Constitution between the States so ratifying the Same.

When conventions in nine States ratify this Constitution, it is enough to establish this Constitution between those same nine States.

The Preamble to The Bill of Rights

**Congress of the United States
begun and held at the City of New-York, on
Wednesday the fourth of March, one thousand seven hundred and
eighty nine.**

**THE Conventions of a number of the States, having at the time of their
adopting the Constitution, expressed a desire, in order to prevent
misconstruction or abuse of its powers, that further declaratory and
restrictive clauses should be added: And as extending the ground of
public confidence in the Government, will best ensure the beneficent
ends of its institution.**

**RESOLVED by the Senate and House of Representatives of the United
States of America, in Congress assembled, two thirds of both Houses
concurring, that the following Articles be proposed to the Legislatures
of the several States, as amendments to the Constitution of the United
States, all, or any of which Articles, when ratified by three fourths of
the said Legislatures, to be valid to all intents and purposes, as part of
the said Constitution; viz.**

**ARTICLES in addition to, and Amendment of the Constitution of the
United States of America, proposed by Congress, and ratified by the
Legislatures of the several States, pursuant to the fifth Article of the
original Constitution.**

They're not just Amendments, they're additional Articles. They have
been since the first ten were added at once. They are outright additions
to the Constitution, new sections, not just going in to change some words
in existing sections. An Article is a specific section of a document. An
Amendment means only that it was added later. That's why what's
commonly referred to as the First Amendment is listed here as Article
VIII.

Now, the first ten are from twelve that were proposed by Congress in
1789, months after the Constitution had been ratified and gone into

effect. Of the proposed Articles of this bill, three through twelve were ratified. Five States approved all twelve and Delaware rejected only the first Article of the bill. Five States rejected only Article II. This meant that eleven States approved Articles III through XII, enough to ratify them in 1791. Interestingly, one of those ratifying States was Vermont, which only became a State in 1791, months before ratifying them, and after nine other States already had. Three States, Massachusetts, Georgia and Connecticut, did not add their superfluous ratification until 1939, almost a full 150 years since they were proposed.

Strangely, it was Article II, the most rejected Article at the time, which came back to be ratified in 1992. Article I of this bill, to date, has not been ratified. Only Kentucky has joined the original ten States to ratify it, leaving it still, Delaware having once rejected it, on the table for 38 States, of which 27 would be needed for ratification. It reads:

Article the first... After the first enumeration required by the first article of the Constitution, there shall be one Representative for every thirty thousand, until the number shall amount to one hundred, after which the proportion shall be so regulated by Congress, that there shall be not less than one hundred Representatives, nor less than one Representative for every forty thousand persons, until the number of Representatives shall amount to two hundred; after which the proportion shall be so regulated by Congress, that there shall not be less than two hundred Representatives, nor more than one Representative for every fifty thousand persons.

The amending process should not be taken lightly nor used for frivolous or trivial purposes. Each new Article impacts the structure, function and laws of the United States and its government. Many Articles already added, especially those ratified in the 20th Century, have made major changes to the document which was first adopted in 1787. Great care, study and caution should be given when considering further changes, lest the Republic itself become unrecognizable and suffer irreversible damage.

It is of note that it took just over two years since additional Articles were proposed for ten of them to be ratified and that, since then, 17 more have been added, 12 of which came in the 20th Century, all from 1913 onward.

Article VIII

Congress shall make no law respecting an establishment of religion, or prohibiting the free exercise thereof; or abridging the freedom of speech, or of the press; or the right of the people peaceably to assemble, and to petition the Government for a redress of grievances.

Congress shall make no law regarding or concerning the official recognition of religion or prohibiting the free exercise thereof. Congress shall further make no laws abridging the freedom of speech or of the press, or the right of the people to peaceably assemble and to petition the Government for a redress of grievances.

Please note that this entire Article concerns limits on Congressional authority. It states quite clearly that Congress shall make no law on these matters, but does not restrict State action on them.

First, there will be no official recognition by Congress of any official religion. Congress is also prohibited from making laws prohibiting the free exercise of religion. In short, Congress cannot tell you how to worship. However, this is not a mandate to remove any notion of religion or worship from having any place with government or the people therein. It is most certainly not a declaration of a "separation of church and state" in absolute terms. That phrase itself originated with a letter from Thomas Jefferson, written as a response to a letter from a committee of the Danbury Baptist association in Connecticut. Would that it was written in law, it would be left to interpret it as law and applied as stated. However, it is an explanatory statement from Jefferson on the point of this first clause of this Article to say that government and church should not be intertwined and putting upon men whom or how to worship. In so doing, Jefferson is asserting the need to keep religion free from control by the state, more so even than the need to keep the state free from control by any religion. He wrote, "…that religion is a matter which lies solely between Man & his God, that he owes account to none other for his faith or his worship, that the legitimate powers of government reach actions only, & not opinions…"

None of this requires removing the word God, or anything related to God, from any and all things related to government. From at least the point of the Declaration in 1776, it was clear that these men recognized natural law and natural rights. It is those principles which are recognized. No monument to the Ten Commandments, nativity scene at Christmas (itself adopted as a state holiday, though not requiring any kind of adherence or recognition), nor phrase on a Federal Reserve Note, requires any person to worship or believe in any way. In fact, if the words "In God We Trust," put on paper money in 1963 in place of the phrase "Redeemable in Lawful Money," are your largest worry about the monetary system in the United States, then there is still much more for you to learn and you should re-think your priorities. There is no official state religion declared by Congress. Any restriction placed on religious worship is prohibiting the free exercise of religion, for free exercise itself means that an individual is left to do as he or she chooses and any restriction placed on religious expression is prohibiting that free choice and expression.

There can be no law from Congress telling people when, where, how or whom to worship. To ask officers and representatives in government to limit or withhold personal expressions of faith while in government violates Article VI of this Constitution by requiring a religious test. To cite Article VIII as reason for such a request is in error as this section regards laws written and passed by Congress, not any absolute adherence or command on personal action. No person's belief, in any God or lack thereof, is to be placed in front of another's contrary belief to require greater adherence to one over the other. Congress is directed to not deal in religion, but the individual members are not required to refrain from individual expression.

Secondly, Congress is not to make laws abridging free speech or a free press. To abridge is to reduce or limit. Congress cannot pass laws limiting free speech or free press. This means that any law from Congress limiting speech or the press is a violation. Any kind of communication regulation, as with the Federal Communications Commission, is prohibited from federal law by this section. First, to be a law, it must be passed by Congress. No agency or commission regulation is considered law (See Article I, Section 1). The same goes for court decisions. Only Congress can make laws and any interpretation by any court which takes a law from Congress as allowing a limit on speech or the press is likewise declaring that law as unconstitutional as it violates the freedom of speech protected in this Article. Any claim to the contrary flies in the face of this Article and is nothing more than people making excuses for getting around law to have what they want.

Finally, Congress is also prohibited from making laws to limit the right of the people to peaceably assemble and to petition the Government for a redress of grievances. Congress cannot require permits or tell people to keep specific distances from specific people or place any other limit on their peaceably assembling to petition the Government.

Article IX

A well regulated Militia, being necessary to the security of a free State, the right of the people to keep and bear Arms, shall not be infringed.

A well maintained and orderly Militia, because it is necessary to the security of a free State, the right, or just claim due to a person, of the people, to have and use Arms, the tools and implements of war, from the Latin "arma ferre," shall not be breached or broken.

This can be read two ways with minimal difference between them. Either you take them as two clauses, one stating the need for a Militia and the other that the right to keep and bear arms shall not be infringed, or as two clauses with two descriptive phrases between. In the second, recognizing all punctuation as written, it states that the well maintained and orderly Militia shall not be breached. It also defines that Militia as being the right to have and use Arms and adds the qualifier that such a Militia is necessary for the security of a free State. In either case, it plainly states a right of the people to have and use Arms, states the importance of it and says it is not to be breached, broken or limited – at all.

In no way can this be taken to mean that only something called a Militia can have Arms, that one must be in service of a Militia to have them, or makes any claim of government supremacy in deciding or naming what a Militia is. In fact, to allow such authority and limitations runs wholly contrary to the "necessary to the security of a free State" part. A State is hardly free if the government has the authority to determine the ownership and use of Arms. Rights are inherent and individual, not collective or conditional.

There is most certainly no legitimacy to any claim that Militia refers only to the National Guard, the current, official state run and funded militia. A Militia is a body of citizen soldiers. The National Guard is one such body, but not the only one. Citizens coming together to protect their land or neighbors are a militia. The National Guard, as known today, has only existed since they were federally organized in the Militia Act of 1903.

Article X

No Soldier shall, in time of peace be quartered in any house, without the consent of the Owner, nor in time of war, but in a manner to be prescribed by law.

No Soldier shall take up lodging in any house in time of peace without the consent of the owner. Likewise, no Soldier shall take up lodging in any house in time of war but in a manner to be prescribed by law.

Article XI

The right of the people to be secure in their persons, houses, papers, and effects, against unreasonable searches and seizures, shall not be violated, and no Warrants shall issue, but upon probable cause, supported by Oath or affirmation, and particularly describing the place to be searched, and the persons or things to be seized.

The people have a right to the security of their persons, houses, papers and effects from unreasonable searches and seizures. No warrants shall be issued without probable cause, supported by oath or affirmation, and unless particularly describing the place to be searched and the persons or things to be seized.

A warrant gives permission for search and seizure. Warrant, itself, ultimately means to keep safe from danger and to guarantee to be of quality. It is the requirement of a warrant which protects the right of people to be secure in their persons, houses, papers and effects. Further requirements are then placed upon the issuing of warrants so that they maintain those protections and are not arbitrarily issued without sufficient cause.

Article XII

No person shall be held to answer for a capital, or otherwise infamous crime, unless on a presentment or indictment of a Grand Jury, except in cases arising in the land or naval forces, or in the Militia, when in actual service in time of War or public danger; nor shall any person be subject for the same offence to be twice put in jeopardy of life or limb; nor shall be compelled in any criminal case to be a witness against himself, nor be deprived of life, liberty, or property, without due process of law; nor shall private property be taken for public use, without just compensation.

No person shall be held to answer for a capital crime, a crime worthy of forfeiture of life, or otherwise infamous crime, a crime punishable by severe measures, such as death, long imprisonment or loss of civil rights, unless by a presentment, a written report of accusation, or indictment, a formal charge, of a Grand Jury. An exception to this, removing the need for a Grand Jury, is held for cases arising in land or naval forces, or in the Militia, when in actual service in time of War or public danger.

No person shall be twice put in jeopardy of life or limb, loss of life or other severe physical punishment, for the same offense. No mention is made of being subject for the same offense if facing a lesser punishment. It states quite plainly that no person shall be tried again when life or limb are at stake, not that they can never be held twice for the same offense. In fact, a person may be tried again provided the punishment faced is of a lesser degree, no longer life or limb.

No person shall be compelled to be a witness against himself in a criminal case, nor be deprived of life, liberty or property without due process of law.

No private property shall be taken for public use without just compensation.

Article XIII

In all criminal prosecutions, the accused shall enjoy the right to a speedy and public trial, by an impartial jury of the State and district wherein the crime shall have been committed, which district shall have been previously ascertained by law, and to be informed of the nature and cause of the accusation; to be confronted with the witnesses against him; to have compulsory process for obtaining witnesses in his favor, and to have the Assistance of Counsel for his defence.

In all criminal prosecutions, the accused shall have the right to a speedy and public trial by an impartial jury of the State and district wherein the crime was committed, the district having been previously determined by law. The accused also has the right to be informed of the nature and cause of the accusation as well as to confront the witnesses against him, to compel witnesses by court order to appear and testify in his favor and to have the assistance of Counsel for his defense.

All accused have the right to compel witnesses, to confront witnesses, to know the nature and cause of the accusation, to have the assistance of Counsel and to have a speedy and public trial by an impartial jury. This applies to all criminal prosecutions. It does not provide exceptions or exclusions of any kind. A speedy trial is one that is done without delay. Having criminal cases sit for months or years at a time before going to trial is hardly speedy. All crimes should be tried within reasonable expedition without exceptional variance in considering what is speedy or reasonable. There is no set definition for a speedy trial, however, the time of delay in coming to trial, defining for themselves what is speedy, should be considered a factor by jurors in regard to the case as the courts should have the means to handle the cases swiftly, without prolonged delays.

Article XIV

In Suits at common law, where the value in controversy shall exceed twenty dollars, the right of trial by jury shall be preserved, and no fact tried by a jury, shall be otherwise re-examined in any Court of the United States, than according to the rules of the common law.

In civil cases of common law, where there is no statute and the governing law is set by prior court precedent for the purpose of handling like cases fairly and equally, when the value of the matter disputed exceeds twenty dollars, the right of a trial by jury shall be preserved.

No fact tried by a jury shall be otherwise re-examined in any Court of the United States than by the rules of the common law.

Article XV

Excessive bail shall not be required, nor excessive fines imposed, nor cruel and unusual punishments inflicted.

Bail or fines beyond the usual, necessary or proper limits are not allowed. No punishments of great pain or beyond the ordinary may be inflicted.

The ideas of excessive, cruel and unusual are left open to some degree of interpretation. Levels of punishment must be declared by a court to be of those types. The intent here is to keep punishments within ordinary reason and avoid the need to challenge them in courts.

Article XVI

***The enumeration in the Constitution, of certain rights, shall not be
construed to deny or disparage others retained by the people.***

The list and stating in the Constitution, of certain rights, shall not be
deduced, translated or interpreted so as to deny, belittle or lower the
estimation of others retained by the people.

Quite simply, one cannot point to the list herein as being absolute and
final and assume from it that anything not stated here cannot possibly be
a right of the people. Nothing within this Constitution is to be abused or
used so as to place a limitation on the rights of the people by the lack of
their stated inclusion in this document.

Article XVII

The powers not delegated to the United States by the Constitution, nor prohibited by it to the States, are reserved to the States respectively, or to the people.

The powers not assigned to the United States by the Constitution, nor prohibited by it to the States, are held in reserve by the States respectively, or by the people. This Constitution assigns specific powers to the government of the United States. It also sets specific powers as being wholly out of bounds for the States. Any power not exclusively granted to the United States or prohibited to the States is therefore a power held by the people or by the States. The people will then decide if or how those powers are to be exercised by their own States or not.

This is one of the most important and most overlooked parts of the Constitution. The center of the Constitution is the limitation of powers of the government. There are few and specific powers held by the government of the United States. Article I, Section 8 spells them out. These are the areas in which the Congress is authorized to make law. Sections 9 and 10 then go on to state limits. Section 9 limits the ability of the Congress. Section 10 limits the ability of the States. Anything not explicitly granted to Congress in Section 8 or prohibited to the States in Section 10 is considered held by the people, to be exercised by and within the States if the people so choose.

There are far too many powers outside of Article I, Section 8, currently claimed and used by the government of the United States to begin to list them all here Most, if not all, are claimed to be authorized through broad interpretations of specific clauses far beyond their actual intent, especially those of "commerce," "general welfare" and "taxation." One simple approach to seeing where the Constitution stops and government begins is to start by looking at the president's Cabinet. Surely, if Congress is not allowed to make law in an area, there is no need for a Department over that area, much less one holding secretarial "cabinet" status.

In addition to the Vice President, there were originally five positions under George Washington. There were Secretaries of Foreign Affairs,

Treasury and War as well as the Attorney General and the Postmaster General. Foreign Affairs soon changed to Secretary of State and remained so since. Secretary of Navy was added in 1798 under John Adams. The next secretary added, Secretary of the Interior, came in under President Zachary Taylor in 1849. That's 60 years and only two department additions. It would be another 40 years until the Secretary of Agriculture was added under President Grover Cleveland in 1889. Arguably, some may consider the Secretary of Agriculture to be the first addition beyond the explicit powers.

President Theodore Roosevelt sped up the growth some with the addition of the Secretary of Commerce and Labor in 1903. President Woodrow Wilson took it a step further in 1913, only 10 years later, when he split Commerce and Labor into separate departments. In 1947, President Harry Truman changed War to Army and created the Secretaries of Defense and Air Force. He put the Secretary of the Navy, along with the new Secretaries of the Army and Air Force, under the Secretary of Defense in 1949. This removed the Secretary of the Navy from the cabinet and replaced the Secretary of War/Army's cabinet position with the Secretary of Defense.

In 1953, President Dwight Eisenhower added a Secretary of Health, Education and Welfare. President Lyndon Johnson went beyond any president before him and added two new departments. First it was the Secretary of Housing and Urban Development in 1965, then the Secretary of Transportation in 1967. In 1971, under President Richard Nixon, the Postmaster General ceased to be a cabinet position when the Post Office Department was reorganized into the government agency called the United States Postal Service.

Beginning in 1974, under President Gerald Ford, the Vice President was no longer considered part of the cabinet, but cabinet-level. That same year, two positions, Ambassador to the United Nations and the Director of the Office of Management and Budget, were raised to cabinet-level. This happened again in 1975 with the Special Representative for Trade Negotiations. In 1977, President Jimmy Carter oversaw the creation of the Department of Energy and further expanded executive power by moving two more positions, the Chair of the Council of Economic Advisers and the Advisor to the President on National Security Affairs, to cabinet-level. In 1979 he split the Department of Health, Education and Welfare into the Secretary of Health and Human Services and the Secretary of Education. In 1981, President Ronald Reagan moved the Director of Central Intelligence to cabinet-level. The Secretary of Veterans Affairs, formerly the independent agency called Veterans Administration, was added in 1989 under President George H.W. Bush. President Bill Clinton moved five more positions to cabinet-level, beginning with the White House Chief of Staff, the Administrator of the Environmental Protection Agency and the Director of National Drug Control Policy, all in 1993. He moved up the Administrator of the Small Business Administration in 1994 and the Director of the Federal Emergency Management Agency in 1996.

In 2001, the position of Assistant to the President for the Office of Homeland Security was created under President George W. Bush. It became the Secretary of Homeland Security and was added to the cabinet in 2003. This department includes twenty-two previously existing government agencies, including the Federal Emergency Management Agency, which had previously held cabinet-level status.

What started as five cabinet positions, six including the Vice President, has grown to fifteen cabinet positions and, in the administrations from Gerald Ford to Barack Obama, anywhere from five to ten non-cabinet, cabinet-level positions, including the Vice President, to say nothing of the many Undersecretaries or other office positions which may not be officially considered cabinet-level, such as the various "czars" which started with President Franklin Roosevelt. Not counting the Vice President's original position in the cabinet, that's already three times as many cabinet departments as when it started, compared to only two times larger in 1913 when it was ten cabinet positions. In 90 years, the government of the United States grew its executive oversight by five more cabinet positions and up to ten cabinet-level positions. 1913 has proved to be a critical and pivotal turning point in fundamentally changing this government.

Article XVIII

Passed by Congress March 4, 1794. Ratified February 7, 1795.

Note: *This Article modified Article III, Section 2, of the Constitution.*

The Judicial power of the United States shall not be construed to extend to any suit in law or equity, commenced or prosecuted against one of the United States by Citizens of another State, or by Citizens or Subjects of any Foreign State.

The Judicial power of the United States shall not be interpreted or considered to extend to any suit brought or prosecuted against one of the States by citizens of another State or by citizens or subjects of any foreign State. In effect, this removed parts of the judicial power previously spelled out in Article III, Section 2 and added nothing. It removed the ability of States to be sued in courts of the United States by citizens of other States, foreign or domestic, two classes previously allowed suit by explicit language in Article III.

Of the fifteen existing States at the time, twelve ratified it in just under a year to put it into effect. South Carolina's ratification was superfluous as it came nearly three years later. New Jersey and Pennsylvania never ratified it.

Article XIX

Passed by Congress December 9, 1803. Ratified June 15, 1804.

Note: *This Article supersedes a portion of Article II, Section 1 of the Constitution.*

The Electors shall meet in their respective states and vote by ballot for President and Vice-President, one of whom, at least, shall not be an inhabitant of the same state with themselves; they shall name in their ballots the person voted for as President, and in distinct ballots the person voted for as Vice-President, and they shall make distinct lists of all persons voted for as President, and of all persons voted for as Vice-President, and of the number of votes for each, which lists they shall sign and certify, and transmit sealed to the seat of the government of the United States, directed to the President of the Senate;-- the President of the Senate shall, in the presence of the Senate and House of Representatives, open all the certificates and the votes shall then be counted; --

This first part is virtually identical to the original wording in Article II, Section 1. The Electors still meet in their States (note, however, that the word "states" is no longer capitalized and may signal a change in view toward the sovereignty and distinction thereof). The same limitations are placed on whom Electors can vote for in regard to State inhabitance. However, rather than one list of all those voted for and the number of votes for each, there are now distinct votes for President and Vice-President. Each Elector is to mark clearly which choice is for President and which is for Vice-President. Then, distinct lists are made of all persons voted for, President and Vice-President, and they are signed, certified and transmitted in the same manner as originally done.

The person having the greatest number of votes for President, shall be the President, if such number be a majority of the whole number of Electors appointed; and if no person have such majority, then from the persons having the highest numbers not exceeding three on the list of those voted for as President, the House of Representatives shall choose immediately, by ballot, the President. But in choosing the President, the votes shall be taken by states, the representation from each state having one vote; a quorum for this purpose shall consist of a member or members from two-thirds of the states, and a majority of all the states shall be necessary to a choice. And if the House of Representatives shall not choose a President whenever the right of choice shall devolve upon them, before the fourth day of March next following, then the Vice-President shall act as President, as in case of the death or other constitutional disability of the President.--

Again, much of the language is nearly the same as before, but now, should the vote for President go to the House of Representatives, they choose from among the top three from the vote by the Electors, not the top five. This Article does not address a tied majority in the Electoral vote because such a thing is no longer possible as the votes are now distinctly separated for President and Vice President and the same majority of Electors cannot give equal votes to two people for President. Furthermore, the chosen Vice-President is now to act as President if the House has not chosen a President by the fourth day of March.

The person having the greatest number of votes as Vice-President, shall be the Vice-President, if such number be a majority of the whole number of Electors appointed, and if no person have a majority, then from the two highest numbers on the list, the Senate shall choose the Vice-President; a quorum for the purpose shall consist of two-thirds of the whole number of Senators, and a majority of the whole number shall be necessary to a choice. But no person constitutionally ineligible to the office of President shall be eligible to that of Vice-President of the United States.

If there is no winner by Electoral vote in the new, distinct vote for Vice-President, the vote for Vice-President goes to the Senate. However, unlike before, specific instructions are now given for that vote. Like the House vote for President, two-thirds are required for quorum and a majority of that quorum is necessary for a choice. However, unlike the House vote, it requires two-thirds of the Senators, not just Senators from two-thirds of the States. In a Senate of 100 members from 50 States, you need 67 Senators as opposed to having at least 1 Senator from each of 34 States.

Additionally, there is now a direct and stated requirement that one must meet the Constitutional requirements to be President in order to be Vice-President. Before, a person could be Vice-President without meeting those requirements but could not assume the Office of President. That is why it is clearly stated in Article II, Section 1 that the Vice-President would discharge the Powers and Duties of the President, not become or assume the office of President. With this Article, all Vice-Presidents are required to meet the same eligibility as Presidents to discharge those Powers and Duties, but it still does not say the Vice-President fully assumes the Office of or becomes President.

Article XX

Passed by Congress January 31, 1865. Ratified December 6, 1865.

Note: *This Article supersedes a portion of Article IV, Section 2, of the Constitution.*

Section. 1.

Neither slavery nor involuntary servitude, except as a punishment for crime whereof the party shall have been duly convicted, shall exist within the United States, or any place subject to their jurisdiction.

Slavery and involuntary servitude are hereby outlawed within the United States and all places subject to their jurisdiction, except as punishment for crime of which the party shall have been properly convicted.

Here, involuntary servitude is specifically stated apart from slavery giving it legal distinction. In this view, servitude is defined as a condition in which an individual lacks liberty, the choice to determine his or her course of action or way of life. Properly applied, this asserts and codifies the right to liberty stated in the Declaration of Independence. However, the word involuntary also establishes that a person can choose to subject themselves to servitude, just not be subjected to it against their will.

Do note the reference to the United States in the plurality (their jurisdiction) not a singular entity (its jurisdiction).

Section. 2.

Congress shall have power to enforce this article by appropriate legislation.

Congress is empowered to write suitable and proper laws for the enforcement of this Article.

Article XXI

Passed by Congress June 13, 1866. Ratified July 9, 1868.

Note: *Section 2 of this Article modified Article I, Section 2, of the Constitution.*

Section. 1.

All persons born or naturalized in the United States, and subject to the jurisdiction thereof, are citizens of the United States and of the State wherein they reside. No State shall make or enforce any law which shall abridge the privileges or immunities of citizens of the United States; nor shall any State deprive any person of life, liberty, or property, without due process of law; nor deny to any person within its jurisdiction the equal protection of the laws.

All persons who are born[*] in, or adopted or admitted into, the United States, and subject to that jurisdiction, are hereby declared citizens of both the United States and of the State where they reside. Previous Articles refer either to the United States as a many or to the government of the United States as a single entity. Article XX reinforced that the United States are not a single entity, that they are a multitude of States. However, this Article declares all persons who become citizens of those States and are subject to their jurisdictions to also be citizens of the United States. It draws a new distinction between citizenship in a State and in the United States and creates a classification of citizenship tied to the United States as a single entity.

---

[*] Please note that it explicitly states citizenship for those born or naturalized. A person must be born in the United States or go through the process to officially become a citizen. There is no provision made for citizenship by proxy of any kind, no exception for granting citizenship based on the citizenship of your child because he or she was born here. You must be born into citizenship or follow the prescribed law to become one.

A Virginian is now a Virginian and an American. A Michigander is now a Michigander and an American. This is like saying the French are also citizens of the European Union. The States have not been dissolved, nor have they been absorbed or annexed into a single geopolitical area. We've simply brought forward an idea that says they may as well have been. The government of the United States is still limited by the Constitution. This does not create a new, overriding authority. It simply adds a concept that moves the States and people away from the recognition of federalism and affirming sovereignty toward one of nationalism with a single, national identity. It does not eliminate federalism or sovereignty. It creates a new identity which changes the terminology at play and begins to undermine the understanding of federalism and sovereignty.

After creating the classification of United States citizens, the States are now forbidden from making or enforcing laws which would reduce or lessen the privileges or immunities of those citizens. This part does infringe on the States as it assumes that United States citizenship trumps State citizenship and that any law which would have been previously allowed in a State as not violating the Articles of the Constitution is now unconstitutional if it reduces or lessens the privileges or immunities of citizens. Previously, under Article IV, Section 2, all States were required to treat citizens of other States the same as their own citizens. They could not pass laws infringing on privileges or immunities of citizens of others States, treating them differently from their own. Now, all citizens are declared to be citizens of the United States and no State can enact laws like that on even their own citizens. What those privileges and immunities entail depends on stated law at any given time. If the government of the United States declares certain privileges or immunities for citizens of the United States, no State can pass a law denying them in any way. The one remaining caveat of protection for the States is that the government is still bound by the stated powers given to it within the Constitution. The government of the United States cannot create powers and privileges out of nowhere.

It is also important to note that this Article explicitly says privileges and immunities. It does not say rights. It also does not say anything about an idea of incorporation, that, somehow, all rules set forth as applying to Congress now apply to the States as well. Nothing here now extends any Congress-only provision to applying to the States. That is an interpretation which, like most great changes to the meaning of this Constitution, has only been taken since the early 20th Century. Any Article which previously applied only to Congress, unless it speaks directly and explicitly to individual privileges or immunities, still applies only to Congress. Likewise, any Article which speaks to individual rights, such as Articles IX, XI, XIII and XIV, still applies to the people individually for the protection of their rights and is in no way hindered or augmented by this Article. This is not an "anything which applies to Congress now applies to the States" clause, much less one subject to the need of interpretation and application by a court.

The next part, stating that States cannot deprive any person of life, liberty or property without due process of law is actually redundant. Article XII already established that. It says no person is to be deprived those things without due process. It does not say only Congress is forbidden from making those laws or that the government of the United States cannot deprive them. It firmly states the right of all people to due process. Stating outright and directly that States cannot deprive them only serves to purposely misread the prior Article to apply it in a certain way, showing selective interpretation, and to further assert here an idea of supremacy over the States. The real idea in action here is the United States directly telling the States that they cannot do something.

To say that no State may deny to any person within its jurisdiction the equal protection of the laws largely reiterates the ideas already stated in Article IV, Section 2 and the previous language in this Article. Beyond that, the significance of this statement is in its exact wording, "equal protection of the laws." It succinctly summarizes earlier terms and broadens the scope some. Equal protection of laws means that all laws must apply to and treat all people equally. States are not allowed to pass laws which apply specifically to any one person or group of persons. They also may not selectively apply laws to any person or persons.

It does not, however, forbid the government of the United States from denying an absolute equal treatment under law. There is nothing here which protects against selective application of law by Congress. Any protections from Congress are stated elsewhere in the Constitution. This protects the people from the States, but subjects the people and the States to the government of the United States. Again, the one remaining caveat of protection for the people and the States is that the government is still bound by the stated powers given to it within the Constitution.

Section. 2.

Representatives shall be apportioned among the several States according to their respective numbers, counting the whole number of persons in each State, excluding Indians not taxed. But when the right to vote at any election for the choice of electors for President and Vice-President of the United States, Representatives in Congress, the Executive and Judicial officers of a State, or the members of the Legislature thereof, is denied to any of the male inhabitants of such State, being twenty-one years of age, and citizens of the United States, or in any way abridged, except for participation in rebellion, or other crime, the basis of representation therein shall be reduced in the proportion which the number of such male citizens shall bear to the whole number of male citizens twenty-one years of age in such State.

A word change from Article I, Section 2 now applies the counting for determining representation apportionment to all people except any Indians who are not taxed. However, when you consider that Article XX already abolished slavery, the Article I provisions of designating free persons and all other persons, with the latter constituting only slaves, and counting them as three fifths, become wholly irrelevant as now the original language applies to everyone and all people are counted equally. Thus, the only real purpose to this language is to affect population counts for representation purposes, but not taxation, if this Article was ratified but Article XX was not. With the ratification of Article XX, this language is rather redundant.

Now, when the right to vote at any election, from Electors for President and Vice-President down to members of the State Legislature, is denied to any male inhabitant of that State who is twenty-one years of age and a citizen of the United States (established earlier in this Article), or their right is abridged or limited in any way except for reason of participation in rebellion or other crime, the basis of representation shall be reduced in proportion of such male citizens denied or abridged to the whole number of male citizens twenty-one years of age in that State. Basically, if a male citizen of the United States, twenty-one years or older, is denied his vote for any reason other than participation in rebellion or other crime, that State's representation count shall be reduced accordingly. This means you can only deny them their vote on the basis of rebellion or other crime and not have it affect your representation count. Any other denial or abridgement of vote penalizes the State's population count. Say your State has a population of 500,000 people. Ordinarily, that is your counted population. However, say you have 240,000 men age twenty-one or older, eligible to vote, but 60,000 of them have been denied their vote for reasons other than rebellion or other crimes; that's 25% of them. Resultantly, your population count is cut by 25% and, officially, your State is recorded as having 375,000, not 500,000, all because you denied a vote to 60,000.

However, it should be noted that nothing here established a right of anyone to vote. The statements made are qualifications placed on population count in regard to the conduct of voting in a State. It does not outright state that all citizens have a right to vote. It does not say that all men age twenty-one or older have a right to vote. If anything, use of the word "right" at the beginning is a slight misnomer. It calls voting a right, but then reacts to qualifications on that voting. It does not serve to open voting to all people or all citizens. In fact, it only establishes a penalty for denying a vote to a specific category of people, men twenty-one or older, for reasons other than rebellion or crime. There is nothing here to say it matters if a man under twenty-one votes or if any woman votes at all.

It does not say that a right to vote shall not be denied or infringed. At most, it implies that only men twenty-one and over may vote, or are at least expected to be allowed to vote. Article I, Section 4, leaves election law up to the State Legislatures. Any State, if they wish, can allow whom they choose to vote. The ability to prescribe that by law establishes voting as a privilege of recognized citizenship, not an absolute and inherent right. Consider this penalty provision to be a forerunner of later laws whereby Congress tells the States that they must comply with something or else lose something else, like tying seat belt laws to transportation funding. No one is saying the States must allow all men twenty-one and older to vote, just that their population count for Congressional representation will be hurt if they don't. Twenty-eight States agreed to those terms and ratified it. Of course, by not declaring a right to a vote, none of this really means anything. You can't deny a right that does not exist, thus there can be no punishment for denying it. If a State recognizes voting as a right, then it's got teeth.

Section. 3.

No person shall be a Senator or Representative in Congress, or elector of President and Vice-President, or hold any office, civil or military, under the United States, or under any State, who, having previously taken an oath, as a member of Congress, or as an officer of the United States, or as a member of any State legislature, or as an executive or judicial officer of any State, to support the Constitution of the United States, shall have engaged in insurrection or rebellion against the same, or given aid or comfort to the enemies thereof. But Congress may by a vote of two-thirds of each House, remove such disability.

No person shall hold any office, civil or military, under the United States or any State, if they, having previously taken an oath, as a legislator, judicial officer, executive or other officer of the United States or any State, to support the Constitution of the United States, have engaged in insurrection or rebellion against the Constitution of the United States or given aid or comfort to its enemies. Congress may make exceptions to this by a two-thirds vote of each House.

The intent here is to bar those who have sworn an oath to support the Constitution and then acted against the United States from holding another office. However, the wording says they need to have engaged against the Constitution or aided its enemies, which isn't quite nearly the same as engaging against the United States or its government or aided the enemies of either. Even so, with its exception making ability, in 1898 Congress issued a general, non-specific exemption for all people, effectively nullifying this section. This didn't require another amendment because they're empowered to make those exemptions and there is no stated limitation saying it can't be one, sweeping exemption.

Section. 4.

The validity of the public debt of the United States, authorized by law, including debts incurred for payment of pensions and bounties for services in suppressing insurrection or rebellion, shall not be questioned. But neither the United States nor any State shall assume or pay any debt or obligation incurred in aid of insurrection or rebellion against the United States, or any claim for the loss or emancipation of any slave; but all such debts, obligations and claims shall be held illegal and void.

The validity of the public debt of the United States, which includes debts for pension payments and bounties for services in suppressing insurrection or rebellion, shall not be questioned. The validity of the debt of the United States shall not be questioned. Article I, Section 8 authorizes Congress to lay and collect taxes to pay debts of the United States. Article VI takes on the debts from before the Constitution. It may just be a matter of semantics here, but it is unclear if the United States named in this section refers to the States together, as it did in Articles I and VI, or if all uses of those words now mean the United States as one place, as started by Section 1 of this Article. Either way, stating that the debt shall not be questioned goes a bit far.

It's followed by wiping the existence of any debts owed for actions which aided insurrection or rebellion against the United States. Declaring that neither the individual States nor the United States shall assume or pay the debts is one thing. That says "not our problem." However, declaring them all illegal and void goes a bit far. If North Carolina owes money to some of its people, regardless of why, shouldn't North Carolina be obligated to pay? Without arguing here the legitimacy issue of secession, so long as North Carolina stays out of the United States, that holds true. So long as North Carolina is in the United States, the United States has declared that it owes nothing. That's hardly a welcome into the fold for the people who are owed.

Section. 5.

The Congress shall have the power to enforce, by appropriate legislation, the provisions of this article.

Congress is empowered to write suitable and proper laws for the enforcement of this Article.

Article XXII

Passed by Congress February 26, 1869. Ratified February 3, 1870.

Section. 1.

The right of citizens of the United States to vote shall not be denied or abridged by the United States or by any State on account of race, color, or previous condition of servitude—

The right of citizens of the United States to vote shall not be denied or in any way limited by the United States or by any State for reasons of race, color or previous condition of servitude.

This Article exercises Congressional authority under Article I, Section 4 to further set election law that would otherwise be left to the States.

As with the previous section, nothing here establishes voting as a right. It does not say that a right to vote shall not be denied or infringed. What it does say is that citizens of the United States, who are each citizens of one of the States, shall not have their right to vote taken from them at all for the reasons given here, those being race, color or previous servitude. Again, if a State recognizes voting as a right, then the citizens within that State are protected by this to the degree given here. However, by stating specifics, it leaves the implication open that voting is not an inherent right and that other limitations are permissible. To be an inherent right, recognized as such, the right must be acknowledged and allowed equally for all people. That is not the case with voting.

Section. 2.

The Congress shall have the power to enforce this article by appropriate legislation.

Congress is empowered to write suitable and proper laws for the enforcement of this Article.

Article XXIII

Passed by Congress July 2, 1909. Ratified February 3, 1913.

Note: *This Article modified Article I, Section 9, of the Constitution.*

The Congress shall have power to lay and collect taxes on incomes, from whatever source derived, without apportionment among the several States, and without regard to any census or enumeration.

The Congress shall have power to establish and collect taxes on money made through business or labor, from whatever place of origin received or obtained, without allocation in equal portions among the several States and without regard to any census or other counting.

In short, Congress was given the power to tax the money made on business and production without any guarantee of it being equal in all States or in any way evenly divided among the people. This, of course, goes in stark contrast to its original taxing power which was required to be equal according to the census count, meaning equal between each State or individual depending upon to which it was applied.

Article I, Section 8 established Congressional power to tax. Article I, Section 9 stipulated that all direct taxes must be proportional. This new Article, while implementing, but not establishing, the specific power to tax income (sustained by the supreme Court of the United States in *Stanton v. Baltic Mining Co.*, as it "conferred no new power of taxation."), removes that qualifier from Section 9, but only in regard to an income tax, a tax on the money made through business. Any other tax is still bound by the rules of apportionment and uniformity among the States. Taxes on manufacturing, sales, property and anything else must still be uniform.

This wasn't the first attempt at an income tax in the United States, just the most successful one (see "The Origin of the Income Tax" by Adam Young on mises.org). It has still been met with many challenges, the most prevalent being a claim that it was never properly ratified; questions of statehood, language discrepancies and improperly recorded votes. To begin, it is true that Ohio, the 10th State to ratify the Article, was not a State[†] when it did so, but this does not impact the overall ratification of the Article. Six more states ratified it than were necessary. Through February 3rd, 1913, 38 States (37 discounting Ohio) had ratified it and only 36 were needed, so Ohio's statehood has no bearing on the legitimacy of this Article.

Another argument, over the technicality of language, is that States did not ratify the exact, same document and thus ratification was invalid. Other challenges raised focus on the recording of ratification votes, that some States which denied the Article were recorded as approving it.

Multiple books have been written about this Article's validity or lack thereof. That said, it is important to note that this was the first amendment ratified in over 40 years and marked a significant change in government power and its ascending growth over the next century.

[†] Prior to Ohio, States had either been accepted after having already formed their own governments, such as with Vermont and Tennessee, or by authorization of Congress that one be formed from within an exiting State, such as with Kentucky (Article IV, Section 3). After Ohio, starting with Louisiana, Congress would grant an Enabling Act for permission for the formation of a State government in new territory and require giving its final approval, once it was formed, with an Admission Act. Ohio was formed as an entirely new State out of territorial lands, granted an Enabling Act, but had no Admission Act of approval. In 1953, a bill was passed and signed declaring Ohio as a State and giving it official recognition retroactive to 1803, the time of its informally assumed statehood. Unfortunately, retroactive laws take effect after the fact, or ex post facto, and are expressly forbidden by Article I, Section 9. In effect, Ohio has still not been formally granted admission as a State.

Article XXIV

Passed by Congress May 13, 1912. Ratified April 8, 1913.

Note: *This Article modified Article I, Section 3, of the Constitution.*

The Senate of the United States shall be composed of two Senators from each State, elected by the people thereof, for six years; and each Senator shall have one vote. The electors in each State shall have the qualifications requisite for electors of the most numerous branch of the State legislatures.

The Senate of the United States shall have two Senators from each State, elected by the people of that State for six years. Each Senator shall have one vote. Electors, meanings voters, in each State, shall have the qualifications required to vote for the branch of their State legislature with the most members.

The first part of that is what people are familiar with. It takes the selection of Senators out of the hands of State legislatures, thereby stripping the States of their check on authority in the Congress, and makes all of Congress publicly elected. No longer would there be Senators appointed by the States to argue on behalf of the States. Everything becomes about elections and "the people." That's the second, consecutive, significant change in government power in 1913. First they changed the power of direct taxation to make it more expedient, then, subsequently stripped the States of their checks in Congress. That's two reversals of original intent and structure ratified into law in the same year.

Now, the second part of this first clause is easily assumed to mean the qualifications to elect Senators must match the qualifications to elect members of the largest State House. However, that's not exactly what it says. In effect, it declares that all electors, not electors of Senators, shall now meet the qualification standards to elect members of the largest State House. The State sets the minimum standard to be an eligible voter by setting the standard to elect that House and this makes it the new standard for all voters for all elections. It's what it says.

When vacancies happen in the representation of any State in the Senate, the executive authority of such State shall issue writs of election to fill such vacancies: Provided, That the legislature of any State may empower the executive thereof to make temporary appointments until the people fill the vacancies by election as the legislature may direct.

When there is a vacancy in a State's representation in the Senate, the executive authority of that State, not just the Executive as before, must call for an election to fill the vacancy. This is on condition that the legislature of that State may empower the executive of that State to make temporary appointments until the vacancy is filled by an election of the people as directed by the legislature.

It used to be up to the State legislature to fill a vacancy and the Executive of the State could make a temporary appointment if the vacancy occurred while the legislature was in recess. Now the executive authority, which could enable the Executive to delegate to someone else in that branch of State government, is commanded by Congress to call for a special election, but only insofar as the State legislature has empowered the executive, the specific executive office of the State, to make temporary appointments until the time of election. A provided B means A conditional upon B. If the legislature does not empower the executive to make temporary appointments, the entire clause is void and the seat remains vacant until the time of the next regular election for it.

This amendment shall not be so construed as to affect the election or term of any Senator chosen before it becomes valid as part of the Constitution.

No parts of this amendment shall be taken to mean it has any effect on the election or term of any Senator chosen before it becomes valid as part of the Constitution. This new amendment, once ratified as a new Article, applies only to future terms and elections of Senators.

Article XXV

Passed by Congress December 18, 1917. Ratified January 16, 1919. Repealed by Article XXVIII.

Section. 1.

After one year from the ratification of this article the manufacture, sale, or transportation of intoxicating liquors within, the importation thereof into, or the exportation thereof from the United States and all territory subject to the jurisdiction thereof for beverage purposes is hereby prohibited.

One year after the ratification of this article, the manufacture, sale or transportation of intoxicating liquors within, the importation of them to, and the exportation of them from, the United States and all territory subject to the jurisdiction of the United States for beverage purposes is prohibited.

It's a good thing this got repealed and not just because prohibition doesn't work. Making exportation illegal is redundant if you already made manufacture and sale illegal. A ban on importation to is redundant after you ban transportation within. Finally, the idea of a territory being "subject to the jurisdiction of the United States for beverage purposes" is odd. This banned all alcohol, not just for beverage purposes. Beverage purposes, as written, only enter into this in regard to territory jurisdiction, territories subject to jurisdiction for beverage purposes. This could be taken to mean that any beverage law enforced in international trade makes that territory subject to jurisdiction for beverage purposes and this thereby bans alcohol there too.

Section. 2.

The Congress and the several States shall have concurrent power to enforce this article by appropriate legislation.

The Congress and the several States shall have equal, simultaneous power to enforce this article by appropriate legislation.

Unlike most areas of law, which are left up to one or the other, the Congress or the States, this is meant to be an absolute ban and both Congress and the States are able to legislate as they see fit to enforce that ban. The only condition to these laws, not stated here, but certainly implied, is that they cannot violate other laws. They can supersede them, depending on which laws they are and from whose authority, but they cannot outright violate a law they are not able to supersede.

Section. 3.

This article shall be inoperative unless it shall have been ratified as an amendment to the Constitution by the legislatures of the several States, as provided in the Constitution, within seven years from the date of the submission hereof to the States by the Congress.

This article shall not be in effect unless it shall have been ratified as an amendment to the Constitution by the legislatures of the several States, as outlined in the Constitution, within seven years of the date from when it is submitted by the Congress to the States.

Unless stated otherwise, proposed amendments have an unlimited shelf life and never expire. One of the first twelve proposed is technically still open for ratification. You simply need the right number of States to ratify it. That number, of course, increases as the number of States increases. This article, however, was specifically given seven years to be ratified. It took barely thirteen months to be done. It was the third new article to be ratified and added since the start of 1913. That's three new articles inside of just under six years.

Article XXVI

Passed by Congress June 4, 1919. Ratified August 18, 1920.

The right of citizens of the United States to vote shall not be denied or abridged by the United States or by any State on account of sex.

The right of citizens of the United States to vote shall not be denied or limited by the United States or by any State on account of the structural and functional differences by which the male and female are distinguished.

This Article exercises Congressional authority under Article I, Section 4 to further set election law that would otherwise be left to the States.

This is, almost verbatim, the same as Article XXII. The only difference is the exact stipulation being laid out. This says that citizens of the United States shall not be denied their right to vote simply on the basis of being a man or a woman.

However, there is still nothing to establish an absolute right to a vote. If voting is an absolute right, there would be no need to spell out specific things for which the right cannot be denied. Rights can only be justly denied as punishment for a crime and even that is an idea not to be taken lightly. What has been established here is one reason for which voting cannot be denied while voting is errantly called a right but not treated as one. It does not even guarantee women can vote, just that they cannot be denied on the basis of being a woman.

Congress shall have power to enforce this article by appropriate legislation.

Congress is empowered to write suitable and proper laws for the enforcement of this Article.

Article XXVII

Passed by Congress March 2, 1932. Ratified January 23, 1933.

Note: *Section 2 of this Article modified Article I, Section 4, of the Constitution and Section 3 supersedes a portion of Article XIX.*

Section. 1.

The terms of the President and the Vice President shall end at noon on the 20th day of January, and the terms of Senators and Representatives at noon on the 3d day of January, of the years in which such terms would have ended if this article had not been ratified; and the terms of their successors shall then begin.

The terms of the President and Vice President shall end at noon on January 20th and the terms of Senators and Representatives at noon on January 3rd, each in the year in which such terms would have ended if this article had not been ratified. The terms of each of their successors shall also begin at these times.

The entirety of this section simply establishes an official start and end of terms for the President, Vice President and members of Congress.

Section. 2.

The Congress shall assemble at least once in every year, and such meeting shall begin at noon on the 3d day of January, unless they shall by law appoint a different day.

Congress shall assemble at least once every year and that meeting shall begin at noon on January 3rd unless Congress, by law, appoints a different day.

Article I, Section 4, Congress' mandated annual meeting, is hereby changed from the first Monday in December to January 3rd to coincide with the previous section of this Article, though Congress may still appoint a different day by law.

Section. 3.

If, at the time fixed for the beginning of the term of the President, the President elect shall have died, the Vice President elect shall become President. If a President shall not have been chosen before the time fixed for the beginning of his term, or if the President elect shall have failed to qualify, then the Vice President elect shall act as President until a President shall have qualified; and the Congress may by law provide for the case wherein neither a President elect nor a Vice President shall have qualified, declaring who shall then act as President, or the manner in which one who is to act shall be selected, and such person shall act accordingly until a President or Vice President shall have qualified.

If, at the time the term of the President is to begin, the President chosen shall have died, the Vice President chosen shall become President. If a President shall not have been chosen before the beginning of that term, or if the President chosen shall have failed to qualify, then the Vice President chosen shall act as President until a President shall have qualified. For the case where neither a President chosen nor Vice President chosen shall have qualified, Congress may make law declaring who shall then act as President, or the manner in which one who is to act shall be selected. The person selected shall act accordingly until a President or Vice President shall have qualified.

The first note here is that the word "elect" as used in the Article, either is to be taken to mean "chosen" as it is often used in, but not limited to, theological circles, or it is a grammatical abhorrence. Either way, it does not create any specific title of "President-Elect" as has come into use. There is no title, nor office, of "President-Elect."

Secondly, we have now established that if the person chosen to be President dies before taking office, then the chosen Vice President automatically advances to President. This is the first point where it specifically calls for the Vice President to become President, not just assume the powers and duties of the office as stated in Article II, Section 1. At no time before 1933 was the Vice President to fully ascend to the office of President and even here it is only in the case where the next President has died before taking office. If the chosen President has not died, but failed to qualify for office in some way, or if no President has been chosen by the time one is to take office, then the Vice President acts as President until a qualified President is chosen, but does not become President.

In the case where neither the chosen President nor Vice President qualifies to take office, the Congress may make law to declare an acting President or the method of selecting one. Congress can choose the acting President. Article XIX establishes how the House of Representatives selects the President if the Electors fail to do so, but this further empowers the Congress, in specific circumstances, to name an acting President of their choosing. Once selected, this person acts as President until a President or Vice President shall have qualified for office. It does not say that either needs to have assumed the office yet. If a qualified Vice President is chosen first, it is possible for that person to assume the duties of President while a President is chosen. While it is not likely to happen this way, that is what the law calls for. Ultimately, Congress is herein empowered to write any law they choose wherein they decide who will be acting as President given a certain set of circumstances.

Section. 4.

The Congress may by law provide for the case of the death of any of the persons from whom the House of Representatives may choose a President whenever the right of choice shall have devolved upon them, and for the case of the death of any of the persons from whom the Senate may choose a Vice President whenever the right of choice shall have devolved upon them.

The Congress may make law for occasions when the right of choice of the President has passed downward to the House of Representatives and any of the persons from whom the House of Representatives may choose the President has died. Likewise, Congress may make law for occasions when the right of choice of the Vice President has passed downward to the Senate and any of the persons from whom the Senate may choose the Vice President has died.

Congress is empowered to make law addressing cases where selection of the President has fallen to the House of Representatives or selection of the Vice President has fallen to the Senate and any person from whom they may have chosen, provided for in Article XIX, has died. Taken to its furthest extent, if either of the Houses of Congress is left to select, as allowed, the President or Vice President, and someone from their selection options for that office dies, Congress has authority to make law to determine who fills that Office. Congress can declare law now to address such circumstances. They are empowered here, in the event of these circumstances, to choose the President or Vice President however they wish. If Selection of the President, under Article XIX, falls to the House and one of those top three candidates from their eligible list dies, they can disregard all other provisions for selecting a President with a new law of their own creation. They are so empowered. This renders the selection process outlined in Article XIX to be circumstantially moot. One could only hope that such circumstances are absolutely avoided because not even a protracted court battle is any guarantee of a just outcome.

Section. 5.

Sections 1 and 2 shall take effect on the 15th day of October following the ratification of this article.

Sections 1 and 2 shall take effect on October 15th after this Article is ratified.

A specific delay was set for Sections 1 and 2 to take effect. However, as implied here, Congressional powers appropriated in Sections 3 and 4 took immediate effect. As it was ratified in January, Sections 3 and 4 were in effect for almost nine months before 1 and 2 were.

Section. 6.

This article shall be inoperative unless it shall have been ratified as an amendment to the Constitution by the legislatures of three-fourths of the several States within seven years from the date of its submission.

This article shall not be in effect unless it shall have been ratified as an amendment to the Constitution by the legislatures of the several States, as outlined in the Constitution, within seven years of the date from when it is submitted by the Congress to the States.

Article XXVIII

Passed by Congress February 20, 1933. Ratified December 5, 1933.

Note: *This Article completely nullified the entirety of Article XXV of the Constitution.*

Section. 1.

The eighteenth article of amendment to the Constitution of the United States is hereby repealed.

The eighteenth article of amendment to the Constitution of the United States (Article XXV) is hereby revoked and annulled.

Section. 2.

The transportation or importation into any State, Territory, or Possession of the United States for delivery or use therein of intoxicating liquors, in violation of the laws thereof, is hereby prohibited.

The transportation or importation into any State, Territory or Possession of the United States for delivery or use of intoxicating liquors, in violation of laws thereof, is hereby prohibited.

There are two glaring problems here: First, it's trying to redundantly federalize existing liquor laws by prohibiting that which is already a violation of law. Second, it fails at doing it. Much like Article XXV before it, the desired intent is one thing, but the written law is another.

While it meant to sustain and federalize liquor laws in any State, Territory or Possession of the United States, it, again by way of poor punctuation, has prohibited the outright transportation or importation of anything into any State, Territory or "Possession of the United States for delivery or use therein for intoxicating liquors" if that transportation or importation is in violation of laws of that entity. So, not only is it adding federal redundancy, it's applying to a classification of United States

Possessions which is hard to find, those possessed expressly "for delivery or use therein of intoxicating liquors."

Section. 3.

This article shall be inoperative unless it shall have been ratified as an amendment to the Constitution by conventions in the several States, as provided in the Constitution, within seven years from the date of the submission hereof to the States by the Congress.

This article shall not be in effect unless it shall have been ratified as an amendment to the Constitution by the legislatures of the several States, as outlined in the Constitution, within seven years of the date from when it is submitted by the Congress to the States.

Article XXIX

Passed by Congress March 21, 1947. Ratified February 27, 1951.

Section. 1.

No person shall be elected to the office of the President more than twice, and no person who has held the office of President, or acted as President, for more than two years of a term to which some other person was elected President shall be elected to the office of President more than once. But this Article shall not apply to any person holding the office of President when this Article was proposed by Congress, and shall not prevent any person who may be holding the office of President, or acting as President, during the term within which this Article becomes operative from holding the office of President or acting as President during the remainder of such term.

No person shall be elected to the office of the President more than twice. No person who has held the office of President, or acted as President, for more than two years of a term to which some other person was elected President, shall be elected to the office of President more than once. This Article shall not apply to any person holding the office of President when this Article was proposed by Congress. This Article shall also not prevent any person holding the office of President, or acting as President, at the time this Article becomes operative, from holding the office of President or acting as President during the remainder of such term.

In short, Presidents are now Constitutionally limited to two terms, except those who fill less than half of someone else's term and then may be elected twice to their own terms. Up until this point, a two term limit was an informal standard started by George Washington which remained unimpeded until Franklin Roosevelt.

For legal clarification, this Article does not apply to and include terms currently being served by a President or acting President at the time Congress proposed the Article. Nor does it prevent such a person, at the time the Article becomes operative, from continuing to hold the office for the remainder of the term. This Article will not remove anyone from office when it becomes operative, nor shall a current term count against the eligibility of the current President for taking office again.

Section. 2.

This article shall be inoperative unless it shall have been ratified as an amendment to the Constitution by the legislatures of three-fourths of the several States within seven years from the date of its submission to the States by the Congress.

This article shall not be in effect unless it shall have been ratified as an amendment to the Constitution by the legislatures of the several States, as outlined in the Constitution, within seven years of the date from when it is submitted by the Congress to the States.

Article XXX

Passed by Congress June 16, 1960. Ratified March 29, 1961.

Section. 1.

The District constituting the seat of Government of the United States shall appoint in such manner as Congress may direct:

A number of electors of President and Vice President equal to the whole number of Senators and Representatives in Congress to which the District would be entitled if it were a State, but in no event more than the least populous State; they shall be in addition to those appointed by the States, but they shall be considered, for the purposes of the election of President and Vice President, to be electors appointed by a State; and they shall meet in the District and perform such duties as provided by the twelfth article of amendment.

The District composing or making up the seat of Government of the United States shall appoint in a manner directed by Congress a number of electors of President and Vice President equal to the whole number of Senators and Representatives in Congress to which the District would be entitled if it were a State, but never to be more in number than those of the least populous State. These electors shall be in addition to those appointed by the States, but shall be considered, for the purposes of the election of President and Vice President, to be electors appointed by a State and shall meet in the District and perform such duties as provided by the twelfth article of amendment (Article XIX).

Section. 2.

The Congress shall have power to enforce this article by appropriate legislation.

Congress is empowered to write suitable and proper laws for the enforcement of this Article.

Article XXXI

Passed by Congress August 27, 1962. Ratified January 23, 1964.

Section. 1.

The right of citizens of the United States to vote in any primary or other election for President or Vice President, for electors for President or Vice President, or for Senator or Representative in Congress, shall not be denied or abridged by the United States or any State by reason of failure to pay poll tax or other tax.

The right of citizens of the United States to vote in any primary or other election for President or Vice President, for electors for President or Vice President, or for Senator or Representative in Congress, shall not be denied or limited by the United States or any State for the reason of failure to pay a poll tax or other tax.

This Article exercises Congressional authority under Article I, Section 4 to further set election law that would otherwise be left to the States.

Like Articles XXII and XXVI before it, this Article rules out yet another reason for denying someone a vote, the failure to pay a tax. However, it is very specific as to which elections it applies: President and Vice President (as electors, choosing electors, or any other future circumstance by which people may directly elect the President and Vice President) and Congressional Senators and Representatives, but not any office of State government or below, only these offices of the government of the United States. States may still deny a vote on its own offices for failure to pay a tax.

Section. 2.

The Congress shall have power to enforce this article by appropriate legislation.

Congress is empowered to write suitable and proper laws for the enforcement of this Article.

Article XXXII

Passed by Congress July 6, 1965. Ratified February 10, 1967.

Note: *This Article modified Article II, Section 1, of the Constitution.*

Section. 1.

In case of the removal of the President from office or of his death or resignation, the Vice President shall become President.

In case of the removal of the President from office or of his death or resignation, the Vice President shall become President.

Quite plainly, the Vice President no longer assumes the powers and duties of the President, as previously established in Article II, Section 1. Rather, the Vice President now becomes President, another fundamental change in the structure and operation of government power. Article XXVII only applies to the case of an elected President dying before taking office. Prior to 1967, any Vice President taking over as President was meant only to take over the powers and duties of the President, act in his stead, until such time as a new President is elected, not ascend to being President. This rule applied to John Tyler in 1841, Millard Fillmore in 1853, Andrew Johnson in 1865, Chester A. Arthur in 1881, Theodore Roosevelt in 1901, Calvin Coolidge in 1923, Harry S. Truman in 1945 and Lyndon B. Johnson in 1963. As they were never elected to the Presidency themselves, Tyler, Fillmore, Andrew Johnson and Chester Arthur never were President; they only filled the powers and duties. This means Vice President Andrew Johnson was impeached, not President Andrew Johnson, making Bill Clinton the first President to be impeached. It's an important distinction to make. Why else would Section 1 of this Article have been written?

Section. 2.

Whenever there is a vacancy in the office of the Vice President, the President shall nominate a Vice President who shall take office upon confirmation by a majority vote of both Houses of Congress.

Whenever there is a vacancy in the office of the Vice President, the President shall, not may, but shall, nominate a Vice President who shall take office upon confirmation by a majority vote of both Houses of Congress. Perhaps the intent was a majority vote in each House of Congress, but that's not what this says. A majority of both Houses means a majority of the entirety of both Houses. As Congress fixed the size of the lower house at 435 in 1911 and there are considered to be 50 States with two Senators from each, a majority is needed from 535 to confirm a new Vice President. You do not need 218 Representatives and 51 Senators if you have enough beyond a majority in one to make up for the lack of a majority in the other. You only need 268 total votes. The most narrow majority in the House and an even split in the Senate qualifies. The entire Senate could be against the new Vice President, but 268 votes in the House can confirm him.

Section. 3.

Whenever the President transmits to the President pro tempore of the Senate and the Speaker of the House of Representatives his written declaration that he is unable to discharge the powers and duties of his office, and until he transmits to them a written declaration to the contrary, such powers and duties shall be discharged by the Vice President as Acting President.

Whenever the President communicates, dispatches or sends forward to the President pro tempore of the Senate and the Speaker of the House of Representatives a written declaration that he is unable to discharge the powers and duties of his office, and until he likewise communicates to them a written declaration to the contrary, the duties and powers of the President shall be discharged by the Vice President as Acting President.

Article XXVII introduced the idea of an acting President, which differs from the Vice President assuming the powers and duties in that the acting President is considered a temporary President. This section adds Acting President as a more official term and sets the criteria by which the Vice President becomes Acting President. Section 1 makes the Vice President the new President if the President is removed from office, dies or resigns. Section 3 allows the President to sit out being President and reinstate himself at his discretion by writing declarations of intent to leave and to reconvene the office. A conflict with Section 1 may arise if the

President, in his written notice, removes himself from office, since Section 1 provides for in case of removal and it does not specify removal must be through impeachment and removal by Congress. This becomes a legal grey area as to what constitutes the President being "removed" since it determines if the Vice President becomes President or just takes over as Acting President for a while.

Of course, the bigger issue is that the President is now allowed to, at his discretion, take a leave from his office and also put himself back in office. There is no stipulation for acceptance by the President pro tempore or Speaker for the either letter, only that the President must give them written declaration. One may assume that this power will not be used often or for light and transient causes, but there is no legal provision requiring either. The President can, at will, take a break, leave the Vice President in charge and then come back. Any time the President leaves in this way, the Vice President becomes Acting President and does so until the President returns. Is Acting President a new role taken on concurrently with being Vice President or is it an entirely new role and there is now a vacancy in the office of Vice President? If a vacancy, Section 2 would take effect, except that it is only the President who is empowered to nominate a Vice President, not the Acting President. Had they left Acting President as acting President, Section 2 could possibly be invoked as discharging powers, but the position has now been officially titled. If no vacancy, if Vice President and Acting President are concurrent, then, upon the return of the President, the Vice President is just the Vice President again. If "Acting President" is not considered a title unto itself, then the Vice President, as Acting President, can nominate his own Vice President, but the Acting President is no longer Acting President nor Vice President once the President submits his letter to return to office. This whole section greatly enlarged the authority and autonomy of the President and leaves open the opportunity for a massive legal conundrum regarding offices and titles.

Section. 4.

Whenever the Vice President and a majority of either the principal officers of the executive departments or of such other body as Congress may by law provide, transmit to the President pro tempore of the Senate and the Speaker of the House of Representatives their written declaration that the President is unable to discharge the powers and duties of his office, the Vice President shall immediately assume the powers and duties of the office as Acting President.

Whenever the Vice President and a majority of either 1- the principal officers, not secretaries and generals, but "principal officers" of the executive departments, not just "cabinet positions" or other specific departments, but all executive departments, or 2- such other body as Congress may by law provide, communicate, dispatch or send forward to the President pro tempore of the Senate and the Speaker of the House of Representatives their written declaration that the President is unable to discharge the powers and duties of his office, the Vice President shall immediately assume the powers and duties of the office as Acting President.

As with Section 3 before it, the Vice President can take over as Acting President. This time, it is at the discretion of the Vice President and a semi-indeterminate group of executive officers or another group, if so allowed by Congress. Fundamentally, Congress could declare a group of its own members as this "other body," they agree with the Vice President that the President is to be removed and all it takes is a transmitted letter saying so. In effect, it's a legitimized coup d'etat.

Thereafter, when the President transmits to the President pro tempore of the Senate and the Speaker of the House of Representatives his written declaration that no inability exists, he shall resume the powers and duties of his office unless the Vice President and a majority of either the principal officers of the executive department or of such other body as Congress may by law provide, transmit within four days to the President pro tempore of the Senate and the Speaker of the House of Representatives their written declaration that the President is unable to discharge the powers and duties of his office. Thereupon Congress shall decide the issue, assembling within forty-eight hours for that purpose if not in session. If the Congress, within twenty-one days after receipt of the latter written declaration, or, if Congress is not in session, within twenty-one days after Congress is required to assemble, determines by two-thirds vote of both Houses that the President is unable to discharge the powers and duties of his office, the Vice President shall continue to discharge the same as Acting President; otherwise, the President shall resume the powers and duties of his office.

After this letter instills the Vice President as President, the President can send his own written declaration to the President pro tempore of the Senate and the Speaker of the House to say he is able to discharge his duties and he once again is President. That is, unless the Vice President and the previously established group which removed him from office do, within four days transmit to the President pro tempore of the Senate and the Speaker of the House their own written declaration that, no, the President is unable to discharge his powers and duties.

In short, the Vice President and, forsaking pleasantries, his cabal, can send a letter to remove the President. The President can respond with his own letter, effectively saying "Am too" and take back his office, but the Vice President and his group have four days to respond with "are not." It does not even specify from when the four day timeframe is counted. Since it does not specify four days from the point the President sent his own letter, it could be argued that the Vice President has four days from sending the first letter to wait for the President to send a letter and then respond with another letter.

Once the Vice President and his group have submitted the second letter, it is up to Congress to decide the issue. If not already in session, they have forty-eight hours to assemble. The Congress then has twenty-one days, either from receipt of the Vice President's second letter while in session, or from the point of assembling within forty-eight hours after the letter if not already in session, to decide if the President is able to discharge the powers and duties of his office or not. If two-thirds of both Houses, again, as in Section 2, both Houses, not each, decide the President is unable to discharge his powers and duties, the Vice President once again discharges them as Acting President. If not, the President resumes the full powers and duties of his office.

Congress is herein empowered in this Article to collude with the Vice President to remove the President from office and become Acting President. Section 4 fails to address the post-Congressional outcome of the Vice President as Acting President. No further method is provided for the President to return to office. No provision is given whereby the Acting President's term ends. It is left to assume that the next election takes precedence in filling the offices as usual.

Article XXXIII

Passed by Congress March 23, 1971. Ratified July 1, 1971.

Note: *Section 1 of this Article modified Article XXI, Section 2 of the Constitution.*

Section 1.
The right of citizens of the United States, who are eighteen years of age or older, to vote shall not be denied or abridged by the United States or by any State on account of age.

The right of citizens of the United States, who are eighteen years of age or older, to vote shall not be denied or limited by the United States or by any State on account of age.

This Article exercises Congressional authority under Article I, Section 4 to further set election law that would otherwise be left to the States.

Just like Articles XXII and XXVI before it, a specific standard is set here for voting rights. Citizens of the United States shall not be denied their right to vote simply on the basis of age so long as they are eighteen years or older. This also changes the previous age limit under the penalty provision of Article XXI, Section 2 from twenty-one to eighteen.

Section 2.
The Congress shall have power to enforce this article by appropriate legislation.

Congress is empowered to write suitable and proper laws for the enforcement of this Article.

Article XXXIV

Originally proposed Sept. 25, 1789. Ratified May 7, 1992.

No law, varying the compensation for the services of the Senators and Representatives, shall take effect, until an election of representatives shall have intervened.

No law, which changes or alters the payment or other amends for the services of the Senators and Representatives, shall take effect, until an election of representatives shall have intervened.

Simply put, Senators and Representatives cannot change their pay without an election of representatives occurring before the change in pay takes effect. It also says that an election of representatives must occur. In the first case, the offices are specific titles, but representatives in the second case could be taken as any representatives, not only those in Congress. It's the difference between general and specific titles. In either case, general or specific, an election of more than one representative is needed, but it does not specify that the election must be a full, regular election. There could be two representatives chosen in special elections after a compensation law is passed and the law would then take effect. The only real limit placed here is that Senators and Representatives cannot automatically increase their compensation whenever they choose.

As mentioned earlier, this was first proposed in 1789 as Article II of XII and would have been Article VIII or IX of this Constitution if it had been approved then. By the time Articles III through XII of the Bill of Rights were adopted as Articles VIII through XVII of the Constitution in 1791, only six states had agreed to this Article. Kentucky followed in 1792 and re-ratified it in 1996, four years after it was officially ratified as Article XXXIV. Between those times, Ohio ratified it in 1873, Wyoming in 1978, Maine in 1983, Colorado in 1984, five more States in 1985, three in 1986, four in 1987, three in 1988, seven in 1989, two in 1990 and one in 1991. In 1992, with two more States necessary, five States ratified it in May and one more in June. Since then, three more States have ratified it while five have not. Three of those five are from the original thirteen States.

Epilogue

No claim is made here that this work is scholarly or the result of years of meticulous research. There shouldn't need to be. The words are what they are. The text is taken from a transcription of the Constitution, in its original form, as provided by the National Archives. It is the Constitution as it is written. The Articles have been approached and re-written with a view toward clarity of meaning, replacing some words with their own definitions while keeping the grammatical integrity of the written phrases. The intent is to make the meaning more plainly apparent to the reader. It really is meant to be as user-friendly as possible. From there, some further explanation is given to the meaning and application, especially, in some cases, dispelling and disproving common misappropriations.

Do not just take these words at face value. If something seems unbelievable, look into it. Challenge the ideas presented here, know for yourself, but, be honest. Do not stake your claim on just anything you find which agrees with your view. There's no truth in that. Either an idea stands on its own merit or it does not. As Thomas Jefferson once wrote:

"Fix reason firmly in her seat, and call to her tribunal every fact, every opinion. Question with boldness even the existence of a God; because, if there be one, he must more approve of the homage of reason, than that of blindfolded fear."

To properly understand American government requires a proper understanding of its central structure and laws. It's important to know, understand and apply what it actually says, not just what you think it says, what you've been told it says, or what you think those mean. There will never be a meaningful discussion about policy without a discussion and common understanding about the underlying principles and authority. Shouldn't a government policy be rooted in actual laws? Shouldn't laws point to Constitutional authorization? If you can't point to a law to support your policy, the policy is inherently illegal. If you can't point to the Constitution to support your law, the law is inherently unconstitutional. It really is that simple.

However, understanding isn't enough. Principles and laws must be applied. This is why it is paramount to elect members of government, officers of the people, who are men and women of honesty and integrity, who follow written law and honor their oaths to follow and preserve it. Do not fall for a quick sales pitch from someone telling you everything you want to hear. Chances are they say exactly the opposite to people who believe differently than you do. Even if people disagree, they should be honest about how and why they disagree, not try to manipulate others just to push their own agendas. It's not about politics and it's certainly not about political parties. It's about human respect and integrity, about having an open, honest conversation with and about the American people and their government.

Government has a specific purpose set with specific limitations. It's spelled out in the Constitution. There are specific things government can and cannot do, not just should or should not. If you honestly disagree with the contents of the Constitution, it is your right to share your ideas and work to change it, but be honest and fair about it. Follow the proper procedure for changing it. No ends ever justify any means. If the means are not just in and of themselves, they should not be used. Just as no clean fruit may come from a corrupt vine; no just results come from unjust actions. Do not lie. Do not distort. Read the law. Know the law. Follow the law. This includes changing the law, even to fix damage done.

One preamble, seven original Articles and twenty-seven additional Articles: that's the Constitution. It's already changed significantly since it was written in 1787 and ratified in 1788. Has it been for better or for worse?